Who's Looking for Whom in

Native American Ancestry
Volume 1

Laurie Beth Duffy

Heritage Books, Inc.

Other Heritage Books by the author:
The War of the Rebellion

Published 1997 by

HERITAGE BOOKS, INC.
1540E Pointer Ridge Place
Bowie, Maryland 20716
1-800-398-7709

ISBN 0-7884-0751-1

A Complete Catalog Listing Hundreds of Titles
On History, Genealogy, and Americana
Available Free Upon Request

WHO'S LOOKING FOR WHOM

IN

NATIVE AMERICAN ANCESTRY

VOLUME I

COMPILED BY

Laurie Beth Duffy

Alsoomse Angeni - Independent Spirit

Dedicated to All Of The Native American

Ancestors

Just Waiting To Be Found.

INTRODUCTION

I started publishing the Native American Ancestry Hunting Newsletter as an aid to research. Thinking, since I had been having difficulty finding information, others must be also.

NAAH does not perform ancestry research. I compiled the ANCESTORS ROSTER of names so I could refer searchers to each other in the hopes of reuniting lost relatives.

At first Non Subscribers could register ancestors with us for a monthly fee per name. Subscribers received this service free, for one ancestors name, for the length of their subscription. A registration fee was required for each additional name. There was no charge for the referrals.

I was receiving so many letters and phone calls that I couldn't possibly respond to all of them as quickly as I'd hoped. Giving me the incentive I needed to start compiling this book, which I plan to update yearly.

I decided to waive all future registration fees, but each ancestor registration must be accompanied by the permission to print your contact information. You can register an unlimited number of ancestors, but each Ancestor must be listed separately.

If you would like to join and network with the researchers who have registered their Native American Ancestors. Send a self addressed stamped envelope to Laurie Beth

Duffy/NAAH 3308 Acapulco Drive
Riverview Fl 33569.

I have attempted to make this book
as user friendly as possible. It is my
hope that you will find one of your
Ancestors listed in these pages. If
not, I hope you will register your
Ancestor for Volume II.

In Section I the listings by self
researchers consist of the usual
Genealogical information if known.
Utilizing b. for born, m. for married,
and d. for died. This information can
be followed by a 250 word Family
Tradition: This is the story handed
down thru the generations about the
Native American Ancestor. Each listing
ends with the researchers contact
information.

Some of the listing contain the
information "The following has/have
been located on the Cherokee Rolls
though no connection has been made to
the family." Then lists the names, roll
numbers where possible, and the name of
the roll. This does not mean the
ancestor is the person who appears on
the Rolls. Only that, the exact name
appears in the rolls. If you locate a
similar name on one of the rolls, you
must then compare the background
information to see if it matches your
ancestor.

The author, and the Native
American Ancestry Hunting Newsletter do
not claim that the ancestors listed in
this edition of "Who's Looking For Whom
In Native American Ancestry" are
actually Native Americans. Merely, that
the names listed are being researched

by the listed researchers, for Native
Connections following their own family
traditions/stories. Where there is a
definite connection stated, these
claims are made by researchers, not the
author, nor NAAH.

Section II consists of those
tribes and organizations who are
looking for lost tribal members.

The indexes are designed to add to
your ease in locating the Ancestors
names. For instance if you locate one
of your ancestors, chances are that the
registered researcher may have more of
your ancestors listed which you were
unaware of. So a check of Index III for
other listings by that researcher is
recommended.

When contacting a researcher,
please be considerate enough to include
a self addressed stamped envelope for
their reply.

I caution anyone researching a
native connection for federal
recognition or financial benefits. You
are in for a big disappointment.

If all you are looking for is a
financial windfall, look over your
family tree and start contacting the
Unclaimed Property offices of the
states in which your ancestors lived.
If they died with no heirs, or no will
the estate may be unclaimed.

The state Unclaimed Property
office can tell you about unclaimed
safe deposit boxes, insurance monies,
retirement benefits, savings accounts,
stocks and much more.

Table of Contents

SECTION I

NATIVE AMERICAN ANCESTORS AND THEIR RESEARCHERS

ADAMS

Adams, Anne Jane.

b. 20, Nov. 1836 Indiana County Pa. m.
Finley Allshouse 14, Jan. 1856 in Lamar
Station, by Rev Conner of MC Church.
Anne Jane Adams who was endowed 13,
Sept. 13, 1911. Salt Lake City Utah for
her parents. Taken from Salt Lake
Temple records #9038 Book D IVG., page
252. There are actually three listings
for her, with three different spellings
of her first name. Ann Jane Adams; Anne
Jane Adams; and Ann (Anna) Jane Adams.
All show her married to Finley
Allshouse died 12 Apr. 1923 in
California Pa. Wash Co. Recent contact
with another distant cousin brings
forth another variation of her first
name, that of Annie.

* Researcher: Laurie Beth Duffy 3308
Acapulco Dr Riverview Fl 33569.

Adams, Lydia (Licenbegler, Ostandes,
Pierce).

b.? m. see - Samuel D Adams. Was said
to have had several papooses, though no
information has been found about any
other than Anne Jane. Lydia was of the
Shawnee Tribe, located at the mouth of
the Youghiogheny river. The original
name we had for her was Liceinbegler,
though I do not know where this came
from. When some cousins researched
Lydia's daughter Anne Jane Adams who
was endowed September 13, 1911 Salt
Lake City Utah for her parents. Taken
from Salt Lake Temple records #9038
Book D IVG., page 252. They came back
with the name Lydia Ostander Adams.
Then, when Anne Jane died, it was said

Lydia had, had the maiden name of
Pierce. My brother decided to go to the
local Mormon library in Denver
Colorado, to verify the information on
Lydia's daughter Anne Jane Adams. He
found three listings for her, with
three different spellings of her first
name. Ann Jane Adams; Anne Jane Adams;
and Ann (Anna) Jane Adams. All show her
m. to Finley Allshouse, but list
Lydia's maiden name as OSTANDES not
Ostander. d; along with two of her
daughters in 1845 during an outbreak of
smallpox and were buried where Union
Station now stands in Pittsburgh Pa.
There are no records of the Methodist
burial ground which was dug up and
moved. The family was told and for many
years believed that the bones were dug
up and used as gravel along the train
tracks, Then that they had been
interred (used as mortar) in the walls
of Union Station. Recent efforts to
locate the burial ground have turned up
an 1852 map showing the burial ground.
Also information gleaned from old
German newspapers of the time indicate
not only was the burial ground dug up
and moved once, but a second time as
well.

* Researcher: Laurie Beth Duffy 3308
Acapulco Dr Riverview Fl 33569.

Adams, Samuel D.

b. possibly Indiana County Pa. m.
Indiana County Pa. (see Lydia Adams.)
Samuel lived in West Brownsville Pa for
awhile after his wife Lydia and two of
their daughters died. But no other
information about him or any other
children has been located. A cousin
found mention of a Samuel D. Adams

owning a Tavern in West Brownsville Pa.
after the time Lydia died. She is
trying to ascertain whether or not this
is our Samuel.

I received an interesting response to a
letter I sent to the Allegheny County
recorder of Deeds.

"A search of our real estate records
from the year 1788 up to the year 1880
reveals no listing under the name (s)
Lydia (Licenebegler, Lisienbegler,
Ostander/Ostandes, Pierce) Adams. Other
names checked for ownership of property
included Anne Jane Adams and Finley
Allshouse. Once again, no evidence of
them owning real estate was discovered.
However, there were quite a few entries
under Samuel Adams, but none under the
name Samuel D. Adams. Samuel Adams was
a very common name in the 19th Century
Western Pa area."

In Indian Blood volume I by Richard
Pangburn, I found the reference
material the author used for his
listings of two Samuel Adams' who are
on Indian rolls. Vol IV #2 pp 100 -
111, and Vol X #1 p 40.

Have not yet made a connection, but
there is a Samuel Adams on the Dawes
rolls #10672.

Possbily Shawnee.

* Researcher: Laurie Beth Duffy 3308
Acapulco Dr Riverview FL 33569.

Adams, Sarah b 1779 NC d 1842 Perry
County KY m. Steven Cauldill. d
11/10/1881 Ash County is only 20 miles
East of a Cherokee Indian Reserve.

4

Had a daughter Elizabeth 1800 Ash
County NC.

* Researcher: Lori Brown 6435 Green
Meadow Dr Fayettville NC 28306 - 5714.

ALFORD

b. in the 1800's? in North Carolina
moved my Mom, Grandma & Aunts to
Pittsburgh Pa about 1930. d. somewhere
in Pa, may be buried in NC.

He was a mix Cherokee & Mohawk.

* Researcher: Lysa Jenkins 2025 W
Magnolia St Lakeland Fl 33815. 941 -
683-2948.

ALLEN

Allen, Betsy.

The family name only was located on
page 15 the Drennen Roll of 1852, no
connection has been made at this time.

* Researcher: Lew Roman 277 Inverness
St Broomfield CO 80020.

Allen, Elihu.

The family name only was located on
page 15 the Drennen Roll of 1852, no
connection has been made at this time.

* Researcher: Lew Roman 277 Inverness
St Broomfield CO 80020.

Allen, Rachel.

The family name only was located on
page 15 the Drennen Roll of 1852, no
connection has been made at this time.

* Researcher: Lew Roman 277 Inverness
St Broomfield CO 80020.

Allen, Zebulon.

The family name only was located on
page 15 the Drennen Roll of 1852, no
connection has been made at this time.

* Researcher: Lew Roman 277 Inverness
St Broomfield CO 80020.

ALLISON (or ELLISON)

Allison (Ellison), Susanna.

m. John V Brown in Wilkes NC 12 Feb
1785.

* Researcher: Lori Brown 6435 Green
Meadow Dr Fayettville NC 28306-5714.

ALLSHOUSE

Allshouse, Elizabeth(?).

* Researcher: Lew Roman 277 Inverness
St Broomfield CO 80020.

Allshouse, Finley.

* Researcher: Lew Roman 277 Inverness
St Broomfield CO 80020.

Allshouse, Henry Jr.

* Researcher: Lew Roman 277 Inverness
St Broomfield CO 80020.

Allshouse, Henry Sr.

* Researcher: Lew Roman 277 Inverness
St Broomfield CO 80020.

Allshouse, John Jr.

* Researcher: Lew Roman 277 Inverness
St Broomfield CO 80020.

Allshouse, John Sr.

* Researcher: Lew Roman 277 Inverness
St Broomfield CO 80020.

Allshouse, Leona Lowden.

* Researcher: Lew Roman 277 Inverness
St Broomfield CO 80020.

Allshouse, Mary.

* Researcher: Lew Roman 277 Inverness
St Broomfield CO 80020.

Allshouse, Susannah(?).

* Researcher: Lew Roman 277 Inverness
St Broomfield CO 80020.

ALMOND

Almond, William.

b 1780-80 in Georgia m. 1809 Nellie
Terry in Montgomery Georgia d. 1840 or
50 in St Claire County Alabama.

Possibly Creek.

Had 8 children Tum, John, Rena, Nancy,
Sally, Elizabeth, Rhoda, & Martha.

* Researcher : Nicole Sharpe Assistant
Registrar Cahaba Tribal Association P O
Box 51 Grandfield OK 73546-0051.

ANDRE

7

Andre, Statton Tecumseh.

I have always been told by relatives
our family was related to Chief
Tecumseh. I can trace an ancestor who
was named Statton Tecumsah Andre.

* Researcher: Nancy Gibson RD #7 Box
439 McKim Road New Castle Pa 16102.

ASH

Ash, Clara Belle (Moye).

b 11 Aug 1902 in Hillsborough County
Tampa FL m. to Orion Clinton Ash in
Hillsborough County Fl. d. 26 Jan 1948
in Hillsborough County Fl.

Had 1 daughter Pearl Urshell (Ash)
Wilder.

Possibly Cherokee Sioux, or Creek.

* Researcher: Marian R Wilder 11018
Circle "S" Rd Seffner FL 33584. 813-
621-6780.

Ash, Doris Mae.

b. Aug 17, 1902 in Hillsdale County
Michigan m. Aug 19, 1926 to Everett
Reamer in Hillsdale County Michigan.
d. Sep 22 1980 heart. in Ann Arbor
Michigan.

Possibly Potawatomi.

Had 3 children Shirley, Jane, & Jack.

* Researcher: Cathy May P O Box 6482
Jackson MI 49204. 517-784-8723. email
TAOCAT @ AOL.

BAKER

Baker, Alvin.

* Researcher: Lew Roman 277 Inverness
St Broomfield CO 80020.

Baker, Amanda.

* Researcher: Lew Roman 277 Inverness
St Broomfield CO 80020.

Baker, Angela.

* Researcher: Lew Roman 277 Inverness
St Broomfield CO 80020.

Baker, Arthur.

The following has/have been located on
the Cherokee Rolls though no connection
has been made to the family.

Baker, Arthur #127 The Guion-Miller
Roll OF 1909.

* Researcher: Lew Roman 277 Inverness
St Broomfield CO 80020.

Baker, Arthur Sydney.

* Researcher: Lew Roman 277 Inverness
St Broomfield CO 80020.

Baker, Barbara.

* Researcher: Lew Roman 277 Inverness
St Broomfield CO 80020.

Baker, Barry.

* Researcher: Lew Roman 277 Inverness
St Broomfield CO 80020.

Baker, Benjamin.

The following has/have been located on the Cherokee Rolls though no connection has been made to the family.

Baker, Ben 1868 The Hester Roll Of 1883.

* Researcher: Lew Roman 277 Inverness St Broomfield CO 80020.

Baker, Benny.

The following has/have been located on the Cherokee Rolls though no connection has been made to the family.

Baker, Ben 1868 The Hester Roll Of 1883.

* Researcher: Lew Roman 277 Inverness St Broomfield CO 80020.

Baker, Bruce.

* Researcher: Lew Roman 277 Inverness St Broomfield CO 80020.

Baker, Charles H.

The following has/have been located on the Cherokee Rolls though no connection has been made to the family.

Baker, Charles 1544 The Hester Roll Of 1883.

Baker, Charley #130 The Guion-Miller Roll OF 1909.

* Researcher: Lew Roman 277 Inverness St Broomfield CO 80020.

Baker, Clarence Robert.

* Researcher: Lew Roman 277 Inverness
St Broomfield CO 80020.

Baker, Clarissa.

* Researcher: Lew Roman 277 Inverness
St Broomfield CO 80020.

Baker, Dale Alan.

* Researcher: Lew Roman 277 Inverness
St Broomfield CO 80020.

Baker, Dana.

* Researcher: Lew Roman 277 Inverness
St Broomfield CO 80020.

Baker, David 1775-1847.

* Researcher: Lew Roman 277 Inverness
St Broomfield CO 80020.

Baker, David Hiram.

* Researcher: Lew Roman 277 Inverness
St Broomfield CO 80020.

Baker, Debby Tabor.

* Researcher: Lew Roman 277 Inverness
St Broomfield CO 80020.

Baker, Delcy.

* Researcher: Lew Roman 277 Inverness
St Broomfield CO 80020.

Baker, Diane.

* Researcher: Lew Roman 277 Inverness
St Broomfield CO 80020.

Baker, Dinemis (Dennis?).

* Researcher: Lew Roman 277 Inverness
St Broomfield CO 80020.

Baker, Eleanor.

* Researcher: Lew Roman 277 Inverness
St Broomfield CO 80020.

Baker, Electa.

* Researcher: Lew Roman 277 Inverness
St Broomfield CO 80020.

Baker, Eliza Ann.

* Researcher: Lew Roman 277 Inverness
St Broomfield CO 80020.

Baker, Ellen.

* Researcher: Lew Roman 277 Inverness
St Broomfield CO 80020.

Baker, Emma.

* Researcher: Lew Roman 277 Inverness
St Broomfield CO 80020.

Baker, Ethel.

* Researcher: Lew Roman 277 Inverness
St Broomfield CO 80020.

Baker, Fanny Elizabeth.

The following has/have been located on
the Cherokee Rolls though no connection
has been made to the family.

Baker, Elizabeth #126 The Guion-Miller
Roll Of 1909.

Baker, Elizabeth Cole Bruce #126 The
Baker Roll Of 1924.

Baker, 1869 Churchill, 1532 Hester -
The Baker Roll of 1924.

* Researcher: Lew Roman 277 Inverness
St Broomfield CO 80020.

Baker, Gary Richard.

* Researcher: Lew Roman 277 Inverness
St Broomfield CO 80020.

Baker, Gideon 11-02-1789.

* Researcher: Lew Roman 277 Inverness
St Broomfield CO 80020.

Baker, Gregory.

* Researcher: Lew Roman 277 Inverness
St Broomfield CO 80020.

Baker, Hannah.

* Researcher: Lew Roman 277 Inverness
St Broomfield CO 80020.

Baker, Hiram.

* Researcher: Lew Roman 277 Inverness
St Broomfield CO 80020.

Baker, Hulda.

* Researcher: Lew Roman 277 Inverness
St Broomfield CO 80020.

Baker, Isabelle Louise Darrah.

* Researcher: Lew Roman 277 Inverness
St Broomfield CO 80020.

Baker, Jeffrey.

* Researcher: Lew Roman 277 Inverness St Broomfield CO 80020.

Baker, John.

The following has/have been located on the Cherokee Rolls though no connection has been made to the family.

Baker, John O. 6774 Guion-Miller Roll Of 1909.

* Researcher: Lew Roman 277 Inverness St Broomfield CO 80020.

Baker, Katherine.

* Researcher: Lew Roman 277 Inverness St Broomfield CO 80020.

Baker, Kaye.

* Researcher: Lew Roman 277 Inverness St Broomfield CO 80020.

Baker, Kenneth Levander.

* Researcher: Lew Roman 277 Inverness St Broomfield CO 80020.

Baker, Lancyma (Luna).

* Researcher: Lew Roman 277 Inverness St Broomfield CO 80020.

Baker, Lavina (Luenna?).

* Researcher: Lew Roman 277 Inverness St Broomfield CO 80020.

Baker, Levander.

* Researcher: Lew Roman 277 Inverness
St Broomfield CO 80020.

Baker, Louise.

* Researcher: Lew Roman 277 Inverness
St Broomfield CO 80020.

Baker, Lydia.

* Researcher: Lew Roman 277 Inverness
St Broomfield CO 80020.

Baker, Marion Isabel.

* Researcher: Lew Roman 277 Inverness
St Broomfield CO 80020.

Baker, Mary.

The following has/have been located on
the Cherokee Rolls though no connection
has been made to the family.

Baker, Mary 1545 The Hester Roll Of
1883.

Baker, Mary 131 Guion-Miller Roll Of
1909.

Baker, Mary, A 8204 Guion-Miller Roll
Of 1909.

Baker, Mary A or Donna #134 Guion-
Miller Roll Of 1909.

Baker, Mary E. 7773 4005 Guion-Miller
Roll Of 1909.

Baker, Mary J. 31012 3995 Guion-Miller
Roll Of 1909.

Baker, Mary Maria 1358M Guion-Miller
Roll Of 1909.

Baker, Mary R R128 Baker 1545 Churchill
The Baker Roll Of 1924.

* Researcher: Lew Roman 277 Inverness
St Broomfield CO 80020.

Baker, Matilda.

* Researcher: Lew Roman 277 Inverness
St Broomfield CO 80020.

Baker, Mercy(?) 10-28-1796.

* Researcher: Lew Roman 277 Inverness
St Broomfield CO 80020.

Baker, Michael.

* Researcher: Lew Roman 277 Inverness
St Broomfield CO 80020.

Baker, Nicholas.

* Researcher: Lew Roman 277 Inverness
St Broomfield CO 80020.

Baker, Orison.

* Researcher: Lew Roman 277 Inverness
St Broomfield CO 80020.

Baker, Otto.

* Researcher: Lew Roman 277 Inverness
St Broomfield CO 80020.

Baker, Robert.

* Researcher: Lew Roman 277 Inverness
St Broomfield CO 80020.

Baker, Robert b. 1755 m. ? to Sara (?)
d. ?

* Researcher : Marian R Wilder 11018
Circle "S" Rd Seffner Fl 33584. 813-
621-6780.

Baker, Rodney Brett.

* Researcher: Lew Roman 277 Inverness
St Broomfield CO 80020.

Baker, Ronald.

* Researcher: Lew Roman 277 Inverness
St Broomfield CO 80020.

Baker, Rueben 1766.

* Researcher: Lew Roman 277 Inverness
St Broomfield CO 80020.

Baker, Reuben.

* Researcher: Lew Roman 277 Inverness
St Broomfield CO 80020.

Baker, Ruth Ann.

* Researcher: Lew Roman 277 Inverness
St Broomfield CO 80020.

Baker, Sally (Betsy) Elizabeth.

The following has/have been located on
the Cherokee Rolls though no connection
has been made to the family.

Baker, Sallie E 7769 Guion-Miller Roll
Of 1909.

* Researcher: Lew Roman 277 Inverness
St Broomfield CO 80020.

Baker, Samantha Hathaway.

* Researcher: Lew Roman 277 Inverness

St Broomfield CO 80020.

Baker, Sara.

The following has/have been located on the Cherokee Rolls though no connection has been made to the family.

Baker, Sara E. 31018 3996 Guion-Miller Roll Of 1909.

* Researcher: Lew Roman 277 Inverness St Broomfield CO 80020.

Baker, Sharon Lynn.

* Researcher: Lew Roman 277 Inverness St Broomfield CO 80020.

Baker, Susan.

The following has/have been located on the Cherokee Rolls though no connection has been made to the family.

Baker, Susie J. 17224 Guion-Miller Roll Of 1909.

* Researcher: Lew Roman 277 Inverness St Broomfield CO 80020.

Baker, Stephen.

* Researcher: Lew Roman 277 Inverness St Broomfield CO 80020.

Baker, Thomas.

The following has/have been located on the Cherokee Rolls though no connection has been made to the family.

Baker, Thomas Jr. 131 The Baker Roll Of 1924.

Baker, Thomas Porter 445 Guion-Miller
Roll Of 1909.

* Researcher: Lew Roman 277 Inverness
St Broomfield CO 80020.

Baker, Thomas III.

The following has/have been located on
the Cherokee Rolls though no connection
has been made to the family.

Baker, Thomas Jr. 131 The Baker Roll Of
1924.

Baker, Thomas Porter 445 Guion-Miller
Roll Of 1909.

* Researcher: Lew Roman 277 Inverness
St Broomfield CO 80020.

Baker, Vada.

* Researcher: Lew Roman 277 Inverness
St Broomfield CO 80020.

Baker, Virgina T.

* Researcher: Lew Roman 277 Inverness
St Broomfield CO 80020.

Baker, Walter Richard.

* Researcher: Lew Roman 277 Inverness
St Broomfield CO 80020.

BALL

Ball, Rebecca Hoagland

Circa 1800's NJ.

* Researcher: Summer Storm Box 842
Hernando FL 34442.

BANKS

Banks, Anne.

b. 1825 NC. m. Robert Collins 16 Mar 1846.

* Researcher: Lori Brown 6435 Green Meadow Dr Fayettville NC 28306-5714.

BARNES

Barnes, Lula.

b. 19 Mar 1875 Ky m. James Eales Sharp KY d.1928.

* Researcher: Lori Brown 6435 Green Meadow Dr Fayettville NC 28306-5714.

BASS

Bass, Rice.

b. 1700's in Wayne Co NC to ?.

Had 1 known child Needham Bass d.?

* Researcher: Marian R Wilder 11018 Circle "S" Rd Seffner FL 33584. 813-621-6780.

BOURASSA

Bourassa, Daniel.

And other Citizen or Prairie Band Potawatomi in or near Fulton County In.

* Researcher: Fulton County Historical Society, Inc. 37 E 375 N Rochester IN 46975-8384. 219-223-4436.

BOWEN

Bowen, Lucinda Tyre.

b. 1843 in Letcher Co Ky m. George W
Collins.

* Researcher: Lori Brown 6435 Green
Meadow Dr Fayettville NC 28306-5714.

Bowen, Perin Tyre.

b. Va 1814 m. a Hanner or Hannah.

* Researcher: Lori Brown 6435 Green
Meadow Dr Fayettville NC 28306-5714.

BROWN

Brown, Frances.

b. 11/1/? in Arkansas m. date? to Hugh
Crige Sinclair. d. 1878.

Had 8 children Annie, Emma, Eunice,
Hattey, Hector, John, Julia, Walter
Brown.

* Researcher: Marian R Wilder 11018
Circle "S" Rd Seffner FL 33584. 813-
621-6780.

Brown, Mary Jane.

b. 12 July 1881 Partridge Ky m. George
W Collins in Letcher Co Ky.

The following has/have been located on
the Cherokee Rolls though no connection
has been made to the family.

Brown, Mary J 980 Dawes# Miller#.

Brown, Mary J 5630 Dawes# Miller#.

Brown, Mary J 980 Dawes# Miller#.

21

Brown, Mary J 5630 Dawes# Miller#.

Brown family name only page 37 The Drennen Roll Of 1852.

* Researcher: Lori Brown 6435 Green Meadow Dr Fayettville NC 28306-5714.

BUCK

Buck, Mariah.

The following has/have been located on the Cherokee Rolls though no connection has been made to the family.

Buck, family name only born in Georgia The Henderson Roll of 1835.

Buck, family name only born in NC The Henderson Roll of 1835.

Buck, family name only page 38 The Drennen Roll Of 1852.

* Researcher: Lew Roman 277 Inverness St Broomfield CO 80020.

BURNETT

Brunett, Abram.

And other Citizen or Prairie Band Potawatomi in or near Fulton County In.

* Reseacher: Fulton County Historical Society, Inc. 37 E 375 N Rochester IN 46975-8384. 219-223-4436.

CABLER

Cabler, Mary E.

Adopted by Harris Cabler a white German b. circa 1821 in Tn. m. 1830-1838? to James B Lemmons in Tn. were married by 1838 as the oldest child was born in 1838. d. 1870-1880 of old age? likely in Polk County Arkansas.

Possibly Cherokee.

Had 10 Children - Donna Senora, Ellen B. Paralee, James K Polk, Julia C., Mary, Mihon T., Nancy Eliza, Nicholas, Sarah A Jane, & William A.

* Researcher: Nova A. Lemons 12206 Brisbane Ave. Dallas TX 75234-6528.

CAMPBELL

Campbell, Alexander.

b. 5 May 1844 Brown Co Ohio.

The following has/have been located on the Cherokee Rolls though no connection has been made to the family.

Campbell, Alexander Family G70 The Old Settler Roll Of 1851.

Campbell, Alexander 4467 Dawes# Miller#.

Campbell, Family name only page 43 The Drennen Roll Of 1852.

* Researcher: Lori Brown 6435 Green Meadow Dr Fayettville NC 28306-5714.

Campbell, Andrew Hawkins.

b. Jan 4, 1834 in Tn m. Mary I Stout. d. 1919 in Goshen Ark.

Possibly Creek.

Children Ges, Kst, Onl, Landon, Minnielie.

* Researcher : Nicole Sharpe Assistant Registrar Cahaba Tribal Association P O Box 51 Grandfield OK 73546-0051.

Campbell, David.

b. 1754 m. Charity Yahula. d. 1824.

Possibly Creek Cahaba.

Had 6 + children Ace (Asa), Lacy, Elizabeth, Elijah, Joseph, John.

* Researcher : Nicole Sharpe Assistant Registrar Cahaba Tribal Association P O Box 51 Grandfield OK 73546-0051.

Campbell, Isabella.

b. Oct 1842, in Brown County Ohio. m. 1859, d. 1925, in Brown County Ohio. daughter of Major William Campbell who in the War of 1812 fought against the Shawnee and is documented in "The Frontiersman".

The following has/have been located on the Cherokee Rolls though no connection has been made to the family.

Campbell, Family name only page 43 The Drennen Roll Of 1852.

* Researcher: Lori Brown 6435 Green Meadow Dr Fayettville NC 28306-5714.

Campbell, John.

b. Mar 1842 Brown Co Ohio.

The following has/have been located on the Cherokee Rolls though no connection has been made to the family.

Campbell, John Family G43 The Old Settler Roll Of 1851.

* Researcher: Lori Brown 6435 Green Meadow Dr Fayettville NC 28306-5714.

Campbell, Nancy.

b. 19 March 1819 ?Ga. m. 19 Sept 1836 to Valentine Coleman in Forsyth County Ga. d. 10 Nov 1871 in Roswell Ga.

Possibly Cherokee.

Had 9 children Eligha, Hannah, Hosea, Martha Jane, Mary Ann, Philip Newton, Sara, Susan, William Marion.

It was whispered that Nancy was an Indian. The Colemans lived in the Cherokee Nation. Pictures of my father, Charlie Brown, Nancy's great grandson, look enough like those of Major Ridge to be twins.

* Researcher : Betty B Chapman (Mrs. Charles) 118 Laurel Tree Way Brandon Fl 33511. 813-689-5677

Campbell, William.

b. 17 Aug 1812 Brown Co Ohio d. 27 Aug 1869.

* Researcher: Lori Brown 6435 Green Meadow Dr Fayettville NC 28306-5714.

CAUDILL

25

Caudill, Elizabeth.

b. 18 June 1800 in Ash Co NC.

* Researcher: Lori Brown 6435 Green
Meadow Dr Fayettville NC 28306-5714.

Caudill, Stephen.

b. 1763 Lunenburg Va.

* Researcher: Lori Brown 6435 Green
Meadow Dr Fayettville NC 28306-5714.

CHANCY

Chancy, Rachel.

b. 1725 Maybe NC m. ? to John Reding.

Only known child Robert Reding d. ?

* Researcher: Marian R Wilder 11018
Circle "S" Rd Seffner FL 33584. 813-
621-6780.

CHRISTIE

Christie, Carolyn Isabel.

* Researcher: Lew Roman 277 Inverness
St Broomfield CO 80020.

Christie, John Edwin.

* Researcher: Lew Roman 277 Inverness
St Broomfield CO 80020.

Christie, Louise.

* Researcher: Lew Roman 277 Inverness
St Broomfield CO 80020.

Christie, Margaret.

The following has/have been located on the Cherokee Rolls though no connection has been made to the family.

Christie, Margaret 21829 Guion-Miller Roll Of 1909.

* Researcher: Lew Roman 277 Inverness St Broomfield CO 80020.

Christie, Maria.

* Researcher: Lew Roman 277 Inverness St Broomfield CO 80020.

Christie, Marion Isabel.

* Researcher: Lew Roman 277 Inverness St Broomfield CO 80020.

Christie, William Wallace.

The following has/have been located on the Cherokee Rolls though no connection has been made to the family.

Christie, William 2526 7469 Guion-Miller Roll Of 1909.

Christie, William Jr. 29980 Guion-Miller Roll Of 1909.

Christie, William 29977 Guion-Miller Roll Of 1909.

Christie, William Jr. 3652M Guion-Miller Roll Of 1909.

Christie, family name only born in NC The Henderson Roll 1835.

* Researcher: Lew Roman 277 Inverness
St Broomfield CO 80020.

CLARK

Clark, Iris Lorraine Stewart.

b. July 13, 1917 in Bluff City Kansas
Harper County m. Dec 29, 1934 to Curtis
Ross Smith in Tribune Kansas. d. July
5, 1989 of heart/Kidney failure in
Whiticha Kansas.

Had 6 children Loran, Marvin, Mike
(adopted out), Johnn, Cheryl,
Charlotte.

* Researcher: Lisa M S Peace 813 SW 9th
Ct Cape Coral Fl 33991. or P O Box
150404 Cape Coral FL 33991. 941-573-
0315.

COLLIER

Collier, Dianah.

b. 1820 Va.

* Researcher: Lori Brown 6435 Green
Meadow Dr Fayettville NC 28306-5714.

COLLINS

Collins, George W. Jr.

b. 4 Apr 1876 in Letcher Co Ky m. Mary
Jane Brown.

* Researcher: Lori Brown 6435 Green
Meadow Dr Fayettville NC 28306-5714.

Collins, George W Sr.

b. 24 Nov 1842 in Letcher Co Ky m.
Luicinda Tyre.

* Researcher: Lori Brown 6435 Green
Meadow Dr Fayettville NC 28306-5714.

Collins, Robert.

b. 1804 Hancock Tn. m. Anne Banks.

The following has/have been located on
the Cherokee Rolls though no connection
has been made to the family.

Collins, Robert 2691 8169 Dawes#
Miller#.

Collins, Robert V. 4705 8170 Dawes#
Miller#.

Collins, Robert Warren 4189M 8179
Dawes# Miller#.

* Researcher: Lori Brown 6435 Green
Meadow Dr Fayettville NC 28306-5714.

Collins, Thomas.

b. 1785 in North Carolina m. Nancy
Williams.

The following has/have been located on
the Cherokee Rolls though no connection
has been made to the family.

Collins, Thomas 15636 8149 Dawes#
Miller#.

Collins, Thomas A. 29901 Dawes#
Miller#.

Collins, Thomas E. 32151 Dawes#
Miller#.

Collins, Thomas Jefferson 166M Dawes#
Miller#.

Collins, Thomas Jr. 29904 Dawes#
Miller#.

Collins, Thomas K. 4966 Dawes# Miller#.

Collins family name only page 67 The
Drennen Roll Of 1852.

* Researcher: Lori Brown 6435 Green
Meadow Dr Fayettville NC 28306-5714.

COOPER

Cooper, Mollie.

b approx 1867 in Milltown Ga m. Joe
Moye in Ga?

Possibly Creek, Cherokee or Sioux.

Had 5 children Hattie, Clara, John,
Joe, Mary.

* Researcher: Marian R Wilder 11018
Circle "S" Rd Seffner FL 33584. 813-
621-6780.

COX

Cox, Emma.

b. ? Martinsburg Clay Township Knox
County Ohio m. ? to Calvin Woodruff
probably in Knox County Ohio. d. ? in
Knox or Licking County Ohio.

Possibly Shawnee.

Had 4 children John, Hiram, Andrew,
William Wirt.

* Researcher: Jeanne L Eppley 204 Rome-Hilliard Rd Columbus Ohio 43228. 614-878-4920.

CRUIT

Cruit, Anne Garrison.

b. 24 Oct 1814 Brown Co Ohio m. William Campbell (b. 17 Aug 1812).

* Researcher: Lori Brown 6435 Green Meadow Dr Fayettville NC 28306-5714.

CUNNINGHAM

Cunningham, Carolyn Isabel.

* Researcher: Lew Roman 277 Inverness St Broomfield CO 80020.

Cunnignham, Deborah Louise.

* Researcher: Lew Roman 277 Inverness St Broomfield CO 80020.

Cunningham, James.

The following has/have been located on the Cherokee Rolls though no connection has been made to the family.

Cunningham, James M. 10105 9044 Guion-Miller Roll Of 1909.

Cunningham, James W. 7242 9041 Guion-Miller Roll Of 1909.

* Researcher: Lew Roman 277 Inverness St Broomfield CO 80020.

Cunningham, Richard David.

* Researcher: Lew Roman 277 Inverness St Broomfield CO 80020.

Cunningham, Steven.

* Researcher: Lew Roman 277 Inverness St Broomfield CO 80020.

DANIELS

Daniels, Sally (Betsy) Elizabeth.

The following has/have been located on the Cherokee Rolls though no connection has been made to the family.

Daniels, Sallie 18086 Guion-Miller Roll Of 1909.

* Researcher: Lew Roman 277 Inverness St Broomfield CO 80020.

DAY

Day, Loutisha.

b. 11 July 1840 m William Brown (b. 20 Mar 1842) in Whitesburg Ky.

The following has/have been located on the Cherokee Rolls though no connection has been made to the family.

Day family name only Page 81 The Drennen Roll Of 1852.

* Researcher: Lori Brown 6435 Green Meadow Dr Fayettville NC 28306-5714.

DEMPSEY

Dempsey, Simion Arledge.

b. mid 1880's maybe 1849 or 1850 in
Hampton County SC m. ? to Cynthia
Rosella Tuten in Hampton County Sc. d.
1918 in Huggins Oak Hampton County SC.

Had 3 children Iva Annie, Monroe,
Norman.

* Researcher : Sandra A Ogle 602 Pine
Forest Dr Brandon Fl 33511-7818. 813-
654-9542.

DICK

Dick, Donald.

The following has/have been located on
the Cherokee Rolls though no connection
has been made to the family.

Dick, family name only The Reservation
Roll Of 1817.

Dick, family name only The Emigration
Roll Of 1817.

Dick, family name only born in Georgia
The Henderson Roll Of 1835.

Dick, family name only born in NC The
Henderson Roll Of 1835.

Dick, Mrs. born in Georgia The
Henderson Roll Of 1835.

Dick, family name only page 83 The
Drennen Roll Of 1852.

* Researcher: Lew Roman 277 Inverness
St Broomfield CO 80020.

Dick, Jane.

The following has/have been located on

the Cherokee Rolls though no connection
has been made to the family.

Dick, Jane 25601 Guion-Miller Roll Of
1909.

Dick, family name only The Reservation
Roll Of 1817.

Dick, family name only The Emigration
Roll Of 1817.

Dick, family name only born in Georgia
The Henderson Roll Of 1835.

Dick, family name only born in NC The
Henderson Roll Of 1835.

Dick, Mrs. born in Georgia The
Henderson Roll Of 1835.

Dick, family name only page 83 The
Drennen Roll Of 1852.

* Researcher: Lew Roman 277 Inverness
St Broomfield CO 80020.

DOWDEN

Dowden, Nancy/Ann _____.

b. 1782 (circa) Probably in Kentucky.
m. 18__ William Dowden 1779-1851 in
either Ohio or Kentucky. by 1840
census.

Had 7 children Miami Twp. Logan County
Ohio by 1860 census resided with
daughter Sarah and Shepherd Patton
family.

* Researcher: Betty Daley 8123 Port
Haven Dr. Sidney Oh 45365. 513-492-

0058.

DUNCAN

Duncan, Ida Pinina.

b. approx 1870 in Tn. m. approx 1890 to William Warren Felder in Tn. d. approx 1955 in Missouri.

Had 6 children. Florence, Gladys, Earl, Carl, Alice, Bill.

Possibly Cherokee.

* Researcher : Thomas Adams 4444 Norlina St Spring Hill Fl 34608. 352-683-3831.

DUNN

Dunn, Thomas Spencer.

b. 1869 in KY. m. 1896 to Margaret Virginia McCrory, possibly in Blecherville TX. d. 1919 in Hooker Ok.

Had 3 children Alva, Bessie, & Louis.

Possibly Cherokee or Creek.

* Researcher: Kenneth Dunn 10151 Sierra Madre Rd. Spring Valley CA 91977. 619-670-3396.

ELLISON (or ALLISON)

Ellison (Allison), Susanna.

m. John V Brown Wilkes in NC 12 Feb 1785.

* Researcher: Lori Brown 6435 Green Meadow Dr Fayettville NC 28306-5714.

EDWARDS

Edwards, Elder Norman.

b July 28, 1876 in Eastern Shore Va. m.
Sept 1, 1895 Accomack County Va. to
Dora Catherine Marsh. d April 22, 1964
in Accomack County Va.

Had 5 children, Ollie, Woodrow, Henry,
Mildred & Esther.

* Researcher: Sheila Carr 14912 Laurie
Lane Tampa FL 33613. 813-968-9568.
Pager 219-2789.

Edwards, Esther Matilda.

b Mar 24, 1912 in Chesconnessex Va. m.
Clifford Hurst on Mar 3 1929 in Eastern
Shore Va. d. May 20 1996 in an auto
accident. in Tasley Va.

Had 3 children Julia Rae, Bobby, &
Betty Ann.

* Researcher: Sheila Carr 14912 Laurie
Lane Tampa FL 33613. 813-968-9568.
Pager 219-2789.

Edwards, John.

b. 1812 Eastern Shore Va. m. Aisley
Paulson on July 5 1836 in Eastern Shore
Va., possibly Onancock Va.

Had 3 children John Henry, Easer W, &
James Thomas.

* Researcher: Sheila Carr 14912 Laurie
Lane Tampa FL 33613. 813-968-9568.
Pager 219-2789.

Edwards, John Henry.

b Aug 30, 1839 m. May 12, 1864 to
Esther Ann Williams in Eastern Shore Va
possibly Onancock Va. d. March 11, 1920
in Onancock Va.

Had 8 children Frances Etta, Ida S,
Sudie P, John W, Colie Cincinnati,
Elder Norman, Lena E, & Phoebe Blanche.

* Researcher: Sheila Carr 14912 Laurie
Lane Tampa FL 33613. 813-968-9568.
Pager 219-2789.

ESTECHACKO

Estechacko, Menawz.

b. in TN.

Possibly Creek, Cahaba.

Had 6+ children Menawa, Garra Wynn,
Elizabeth, Bijwarrir, Charity,
Tustanuaae Thlocko.

* Researcher : Nicole Sharpe Assistant
Registrar Cahaba Tribal Association P O
Box 51 Grandfield OK 73546-0051.

FOX

Fox, Amy Ann.

* Researcher: Lew Roman 277 Inverness
St Broomfield CO 80020.

Fox, James.

The following has/have been located on
the Cherokee Rolls though no connection
has been made to the family.

Fox, James 17739 Guion-Miller Roll Of 1909.

Fox, James F. 1553M Guion-Miller Roll Of 1909.

Fox, family name only born in Georgia The Henderson Roll Of 1835.

Fox, family name only born in NC The Henderson Roll Of 1835.

Fox, family name only #60 The Mullay Roll Of 1848.

Fox, family name only #56 The Siler Roll Of 1851.

Fox, family name only #747 The Swetland Roll Of 1869.

Fox, family name only page 101 The Drennen Roll Of 1852.

* Researcher: Lew Roman 277 Inverness St Broomfield CO 80020.

FRANKLIN

Franklin, Elizabeth.

b. 1800 in TN m. Stout in McMinn County Tn area.

Had 1 child Mary Lovina Stout.

Possibly Creek, Cahaba Creek.

* Researcher : Nicole Sharpe Assistant Registrar Cahaba Tribal Association P O Box 51 Grandfield OK 73546-0051.

GARNER

Garner, Mary A.

b. Feb 6, 1813 in Pa. m to William Robbins in Pa or Berkley County Va. d. June 15, 1870 in Center Village Delaware County Ohio.

Possibly Shawnee.

Had 12 children Nathan, John, Henry, Mary, Ellen, Charles, William, Robert, Clarinda, Diana, Amanda, Margaret (infant).

* Researcher: Jeanne L Eppley 204 Rome-Hilliard Rd Columbus Ohio 43228. 614-878-4920.

GREEN

Green, James Robert "Hunting Horse".

b. August 17, 1928 in DeNoya Oklahoma (Osage Reservation). m. October 2, 1948 to Jennie Blelanski in Chocopee Massachusetts. d. October 13, 1989 of Breast Cancer in Marren La. Tribal Affiliation Cherokee Western Band.

Had 2 children Cynthia (Cindy), Shelly.

* Researcher Cindy Middleton 1003 Blann Dr Tampa Fl 33603.

Green, Gordon/Gardener b 1720? in VA, NC or Tn m. 1700's to ? d. 1834 of old age. at the Treaty of New Echota by tradition. Known Cherokee many descendants have been certified for affiliated with Creeks.

Had 6 known children John, James, Iseae, Letha, William, & Sukky.

* Researcher : Nicole Sharpe Assistant
Registrar Cahaba Tribal Association P O
Box 51 Grandfield OK 73546-0051.

Green/Harbeston.

b. August 16, 1949 in Wellsville NY m.
November 29, 1969 to John D Middleton
Jr in Tampa Fl.

Had 1 child a son Chad Trevor.

Tribal Affiliation Cherokee Western
Band.

* Researcher Cindy Middleton 1003 Blann
Dr Tampa Fl 33603.

HAWK

Hawk, Keziah Keziah Hawk.

b. 1821/24 Huntingdon Co Pa. m. Samuel
M Snyder 1844 in Cambrai Co Pa. d.
1887-1900 in Indiana Co Pa.

My husband and I were m. a number of
years when we discovered that his
grandmother, Iva Snyder Beck and my
grandfather George Paul Shaffer were
full first cousins. Iva Snyder Beck is
a granddaughter of Samuel M Shaffer and
Keziah (Kiziha) Hawk/Hawke. My
grandfather Paul Shaffer is a grandson
of same. So I was able to hear
remembrances from my grandfather and my
husband's grandmother. Paul d. in 1984
and Iva d. in 1988.

Iva first mentioned that her
grandmother was Native American. Her
father Samuel Snyder Jr. was one-half
Native American and left Indiana

40

County, Pa because of some harassment
and name calling. When I mentioned the
Native Ancestor to my grandfather, he
said that was true. His mother Clara
Snyder was sister to Sam above and also
one half Native American. Paul said he
thinks that Samuel met his wife Keziah
while he was a fur trader. Samuel
later, around 1890's, had a store and
blacksmith shop in Indiana County Pa.

I have a snapshot of Keziah taken from
a large portrait, before it was
discarded by a family member, who
didn't want that part of the heritage
known.

In 1981, June Lutz wrote a book
entitled "A Historical Account of the
Snyder Family" in which she states on
page 60 that Keziah is Native American.
I wrote to June for the source of this
information and she named Mary Ann
Olinger who m. Clyde Hart as having
documents of proof. I wrote to the last
known address in Miami Fl but the
letter was returned address unknown.

And so while I have no documented proof
of the ancestry of Keziah Hawk. I have
the family tradition which has been
passed down through 3 separate branches
of the family who did not know each
other. And I search on..

Samuel M. Snyder and Keziah Hawk had 12
children: 1) William Snyder b. 1845
probably in Susquehanna Twp in Cambrai
Co Pa. He was in the Civil War and went
West. 2) Mary C Snyder b. 1847 probably
in Susquehanna Twp in Cambrai Co Pa.and
d. before 1860. 3) Elizabeth J Snyder
b. 1849 probably in Susquehanna Twp in

Cambrai Co Pa. m. John J Meckley d. in
Indiana Co Pa. 4) John Hawke Snyder b.
1851 in Cherry Tree Indiana Co Pa. He
was m. twice Elizabeth Rowe and Annie
Adams. John d. 1941 in White Twp
Indiana Co Pa. and is buried in
Rochester Mills Indiana Co Pa. 5) Susan
Snyder b 1853 in Cherry Tree m. Izek
Lee. 6) Lucy Snyder b 1854 in Cherry
Tree. 7) Samuel Sylvester Snyder b 1855
in Cherry Tree. m first Clarissa Rupp,
second Emma Schrencongost. d in 1934 in
Vandergrift Westmoreland Co Pa. 8)
Kesiah H Snyder b 1857 in Cherry Tree.
9) George W Snyder b 1859 in Cherry
Tree was a twin m Clara Sheasley d in
1938 in Indiana Co Pa. 10) Emma Snyder
b 1859 in Green Twp Indiana Co Pa and
was twin of George W Snyder m Martin L
Schrencongost. 11) Clara Snyder b 1863
in Marchand Indiana Co Pa m Charles
Schaffer d in 1940 in Warren Co Pa. 12)
Alice Snyder b 1865 in Grabt Twp
Indiana Co Pa m William Phillips in
1893 in Glen Campbell Indiana CO Pa.

* Researcher: Connie Mateer R D #5 Box
252 M Kittaning PA 16209-8003. 814-257-
8152.

HENDRIX

Hendrix, Carol.

The following has/have been located on
the Cherokee Rolls though no connection
has been made to the family.

Hendrix, family name only page 113 The
Drennen Roll Of 1852.

* Researcher: Lew Roman 277 Inverness
St Broomfield CO 80020.

Hendrix, Thomas.

The following has/have been located on the Cherokee Rolls though no connection has been made to the family.

Hendrix, family name only page 113 The Drennen Roll Of 1852.

* Researcher: Lew Roman 277 Inverness St Broomfield CO 80020.

HOWARD

Howard John or Thomas.

m. a Cherokee with English name of Lettie Durham (or Dunham), 1750-1770's. I recently found a story about Thomas Howard and Shyuica, A Cherokee, in regards to their friendship and involvement in Battle of Round Mt near Tryon, NC. in 1776 in Footsteps of the Cherokee by Vicki Rozema. Family legend says Thomas Howard lived in Washington, Ga but I've not been successful finding him there but have found Howards in Abbeville, SC. He served in the Revolutionary war, registered in Montgomery County, Av and later migrated to Eastern Ky around 1800+.

* Researcher: Becky Gilpin 1540 Natchez Way Grayson Ga 30221.

HURST

Hurst, Clifford.

b. July 12, 1908 m. March 1929 to Esther Matilda Edwards. in Eastern Shore VA. d. Dec. 29, 1974 of cancer in a Baltimore Md hospital.

Had 3 children Julia Rae, Bobby, & Betty Ann.

* Researcher: Sheila Carr 14912 Laurie Lane Tampa FL 33613. 813-968-9568. Pager 219-2789.

ISDELL

Isdell, Willie Estelle.

Daughter of Sula Duckett (maiden name Heaton) and Sidney Duckett. m. Joseph Sherman Isdell son of Pearl Isdell (maiden name Hillsman) and James Isdell.

Joseph and Estelle had 2 children Richard Marlin and Janice.

Richard Marlin Isdell had 7 children with 4 different women, three of whom he was married to, one he was not. the children were Gerri Lynn Isdell, Jammey Isdell, Jacqueline Isdell. Lacey Isdell, Ezekiel Daniel Isdell, Jeremiah Joseph Isdell & Amos Moses Isdell (these 3 sons were all adopted, after Richard Isdell's death around 1986) There was a fourth son (in name only not by blood) Samuel Eli Isdell.

Gerri Lynn Isdell had 4 children 2 out of wedlock and 2 while married Carmen Regina Doucette Isdell, Terrell John Thomas, Pauline Michelle Thomas and Aurasphere Trinity McDonald.

Janice Isdell had 2 children with her former husband David Egge Shawn Egge and Tiffany Egge.

Looking for a possible Isdell Cherokee

connection.

Though no connection has been made the following have been located on the 1909 Guion Miller Roll. Isabell Isbill #1248, Lillie M Isbill #1246, Mary I Isbill #1247, & Sarah A Isbill #1245.

* Researcher: G Thomas Box 369B Nollwood Ln W Bremerton Wa 98312.

JERNIGAN

Jernigan, Mary.

b. 1834 Orange Fl m. to Charles Bass in Kissimmee Osceola Fl. d. 29 Mar 1910 in Kissimmee Osceola Fl buried in Rose Hill Cemetery.

Had 10 children Aaron Barney Cone, Charles, Eliza James, Etta Mary, Joseph, Lucy Ann, Moses Everett, Needham, Robert.

* Researcher: Marian R Wilder 11018 Circle "S" Rd Seffner FL 33584. 813-621-6780.

JOHNSON

Johnson, Anna Catherine.

b July 20, 1845 Hillsdale County Michigan. m. Aug 29 1870 to John W. Raymond in Hillsdale County Michigan. d Feb 26, 1904 in Hillsdale County Michigan.

Had 2 children Amy & Jesse.

* Researcher: Cathy May P O Box 6482 Jackson MI 49204. 517-784-8723. email

TAOCAT @ AOL.

Johnson, Barbara.

The following has/have been located on
the Cherokee Rolls though no connection
has been made to the family.

Johnson, family name only The
Reservation Roll Of 1817.

Johnson, family name only The
Emigration Roll Of 1817.

Johnson, family name only born in Al.
The Henderson Roll Of 1835.

Johnson, family name only born in Ga.
The Henderson Roll Of 1835.

Johnson, family name only born in NC.
The Henderson Roll Of 1835.

Johnson, family name only born in Tn.
The Henderson Roll Of 1835.

Johnson, family name only #203 The
Mullay Roll Of 1848.

Johnson, family name only #215 The
Mullay Roll Of 1848.

Johnson, family name only #1346 The
Mullay Roll Of 1848.

Johnson, family name only #150 The
Siler Roll Of 1851.

Johnson, family name only #479 The
Hester Roll Of 1883.

Johnson, family name only #1158 The
Hester Roll Of 1883.

Johnson, family name only page 128 The Drennen Roll Of 1852.

Johnson, family name only page 129 The Drennen Roll Of 1852.

* Researcher: Lew Roman 277 Inverness St Broomfield CO 80020.

Johnson, Cinthia Ann.

b. 1838 in Mississippi n. to Thomas Monroe Malone in Montgomery TX. d. 1870 in TX.

Had 4 children Berta, Charley, Eugean, Howard.

* Researcher: Marian R Wilder 11018 Circle "S" Rd Seffner FL 33584. 813-621-6780.

Johnson, Silas.

b. 1894 in NJ or NY m ? to Catherine Demont. d. March 12, 1887.

Possibly Potawatomi.

Had 7 children William, Camelia, George, Matilda, Anna Catherine, Alma, & Charles.

* Researcher: Cathy May P O Box 6482 Jackson MI 49204. 517-784-8723. email TAOCAT @ AOL.

JONES

Jones, Alann.

The following has/have been located on the Cherokee Rolls though no connection

has been made to the family.

Jones, family name only #241 The Hester Roll Of 1883.

Jones, family name only page 130 The Drennen Roll Of 1852.

Jones, family name only page 131 The Drennen Roll Of 1852.

* Researcher: Lew Roman 277 Inverness St Broomfield CO 80020.

Jones, Christopher.

The following has/have been located on the Cherokee Rolls though no connection has been made to the family.

Jones, family name only #241 The Hester Roll Of 1883.

Jones, family name only page 130 The Drennen Roll Of 1852.

Jones, family name only page 131 The Drennen Roll OF 1852.

* Researcher: Lew Roman 277 Inverness St Broomfield CO 80020.

Jones, Marisa Louise.

The following has/have been located on the Cherokee Rolls though no connection has been made to the family.

Jones, family name only #241 The Hester Roll Of 1883.

Jones, family name only page 130 The Drennen Roll Of 1852.

Jones, family name only page 131 The Drennen Roll Of 1852.

* Researcher: Lew Roman 277 Inverness St Broomfield CO 80020.

Jones, Melanie Ann.

The following has/have been located on the Cherokee Rolls though no connection has been made to the family.

Jones, family name only #241 The Hester Roll Of 1883.

Jones, family name only page 130 The Drennen Roll Of 1852.

Jones, family name only page 131 The Drennen Roll Of 1852.

* Researcher: Lew Roman 277 Inverness St Broomfield CO 80020.

Jones, Phebe Ann.

The following has/have been located on the Cherokee Rolls though no connection has been made to the family.

Jones, family name only #241 The Hester Roll Of 1883.

Jones, family name only page 130 The Drennen Roll Of 1852.

Jones, family name only page 131 The Drennen Roll Of 1852.

* Researcher: Lew Roman 277 Inverness St Broomfield CO 80020.

Jones, Richard.

The following has/have been located on the Cherokee Rolls though no connection has been made to the family.

Jones, family name only #241 The Hester Roll Of 1883.

Jones, family name only page 130 The Drennen Roll Of 1852.

Jones, family name only page 131 The Drennen Roll Of 1852.

* Researcher: Lew Roman 277 Inverness St Broomfield CO 80020.

Jones, Robert Aaron.

The following has/have been located on the Cherokee Rolls though no connection has been made to the family.

Jones, family name only #241 The Hester Roll Of 1883.

Jones, family name only page 130 The Drennen Roll Of 1852.

Jones, family name only page 131 The Drennen Roll Of 1852.

* Researcher: Lew Roman 277 Inverness St Broomfield CO 80020.

Jones, Scott.

The following has/have been located on the Cherokee Rolls though no connection has been made to the family.

Jones, family name only #241 The Hester Roll Of 1883.

Jones, family name only page 130 The Drennen Roll Of 1852.

Jones, family name only page 131 The Drennen Roll Of 1852.

* Researcher: Lew Roman 277 Inverness St Broomfield CO 80020.

KING

King, Adam Meek.

b. 21 Sept 1838 in Ill. m. 1870 to Ellen Manerva Exell. d. ? in Ill.

Had 4 children Danial, Edger, Marian, Mary Sue.

* Researcher: Marian R Wilder 11018 Circle "S" Rd Seffner FL 33584. 813-621-6780.

King, Mary Sue.

b. 1 Jan 1870 m. in Tx 1899 to Charles Sincanate Mallone. d. ? in Diball Rx Ryans Chapel.

Had 5 children Charles, Clarance, Oceola, Theodocia, Thomas.

* Researcher: Marian R Wilder 11018 Circle "S" Rd Seffner FL 33584. 813-621-6780.

KINNEY

Kinney, Lillian.

The following has/have been located on the Cherokee Rolls though no connection has been made to the family.

Kinney, family name only page 138 The Drennen Roll Of 1852.

* Researcher: Lew Roman 277 Inverness St Broomfield CO 80020.

LEE

Lee, Catherine.

b. Aprox 1700's in Johnson Co NC m. to Mathew Wilder in Johnson Co NC. d. approx 1806 in Johnson Co NC.

Had 3 or more children Samuel, William, Willis.

* Researcher: Marian R Wilder 11018 Circle "S" Rd Seffner FL 33584. 813-621-6780.

LICENBEGLER

Licenbegler, Lydia (Ostandes, Ostander, Pierce, Adams).

See Lydia Adams, Lydia Pierce, & Lydia Ostandes M Samuel D Adams d along with two of her daughters in 1845 during an outbreak of smallpox and were buried where Union Station now stands in Pittsburgh Pa.

* Researcher: Laurie Beth Duffy 3308 Acapulco Dr Riverview Fl 33569.

LOSEY

Losey.

Indian Maiden from Kikipoo tribal area Indiana, m. a Frenchman.

Dear Early Americans. I'm 78 yrs old.
A Frenchman came to our shores in 1700,
m. an Indian wife. This is all I know
of my origin - his wife was from the
Kikipoo area in Indiana. The name was
Losey. My mothers parents were Holman
Losey - his wife Margaret Anne Crowe -
she was bilineal descendant of Patrick
Henry. My 6th grandmother back was
Rebecca sister to Patrick and
descendant of the Henry who built the
fort on which the Statue of Liberty
sits. My own father was from England
Leo B. Lambert - my mother Ruby Losey -
they opened the Cave on Lkt Mtn. Tenn,
the underground falls is named Ruby.
Best info I have.

* Researcher: Frances L Whisler 3405
Kellys Ferry Rd Chattanooga TN 37419.

LOUDERBACH

Louderbach, Anne G.

b. 6 Oct 1864 Brown CO Ohio m. Eli
Mullen Hiles.

* Researcher: Lori Brown 6435 Green
Meadow Dr Fayettville NC 28306-5714.

MALONE

Malone, Andrew J.

b. 1818 in TN m. 1834 to Nancy Baker
Reding in Fayette TN. d. 1840 in
Fayette Tn.

Had 3 children Henderson, Thomas,
William.

* Researcher: Marian R Wilder 11018

Circle "S" Rd Seffner FL 33584. 813-621-6780.

Malone, Thomas Monroe.

b. 1835 in Tn m. 16 May 1861 to Cinthia Ann Johnson. d. ?

Had 4 children Berta, Charley, Eugean, Howard.

* Researcher: Marian R Wilder 11018 Circle "S" Rd Seffner FL 33584. 813-621-6780.

MARSH

Marsh, Charles.

b. 1780 Northumberland County Va. m. May 1 1807 (obtained license band) to Nancy Dameron in Northumberland County Va. d. ? Eastern Shore of Mayrland.

Had 3 children Walter H., Charles D., Elizabeth. There were other children who remained in Northumberland County Va.

* Researcher: Sheila Carr 14912 Laurie Lane Tampa FL 33613. 813-968-9568. Pager 219-2789.

Marsh, Dave A.

b. Aug 12, 1844 (or 1840) Mt Vernon Md m. after Jan 23, 1868 to Matilda A Evans (brother was Capt. Benjamin F Marsh). d. Dec 20 1917 interment in family burying plot.

Had 5 children Messers, D Wesley, James R. Mrs Elder Edwards. Miss Maggie, & Mr

Edward.

Marsh, Dora Catherine.

b. 1878 Eastern Shore Va., possibly
Onancock Va. m. Sept 1, 1895 to Elder
Norman Edwards in Eastern Shore Va
area. d. 1949 of a heart attack in
Accomack County Va.

Had 5 children Ollie, Woodrow, Henry,
Mildred & Esther.

MATHENEY (OR MATHENA)

Matheny, William.

b. c 1724 probably in Stafford County
Va. m. c 1740 to Elizabeth Parker in
Stafford County Va.d. ? Probably
Stafford County Va or Ross County Ohio.

Possibly Shawnee.

Had ? children only known child
Nathaniel.

MCABE

McAbe, Mary.

55

b. 1837 possible NW Utah. m. Sept 6, 1862 to William White d.?

Had one child Joseph White (b. April 9, 1859).

Possibly Western Shoshone.

Mary McAbe was my father's grandmother. We know little about her, except that she was born in 1837, married William White in 1864 at Salt Lake City, three years after their son Joseph (my father's father) was born at Camp Floyd, Utah, and that she was believed to be Indian of that area -- possibly Western Shoshone. Joseph was <u>known</u> to be part Indian.

Although there is no further record of either Mary or William in the records of the LDS Church, records show Joseph was baptized Mormon at age eight at Moroni, Utah, and later married my grandmother Mary Ann Ames at Moroni, where several children including my father, were born. In 1906 they migrated to Chilli, Idaho, where they raised sheep and offered hospitality to Indians passing through the area.

Camp Floyd was an army outpost set up in 1858 near what is now Fairfield, to put down a reputed Mormon revolt against the Federal Government. William White may have been a soldier in that army, may have been from Ohio. Joseph may have been adopted by a Mormon family, a custom of that time.

However, my main interest is in the history of Mary McAbe as an American Indian ancestor, with the hope of confirming my tribal identity, as well as locating and reuniting with present-day relatives.

* Researcher: Donna White 619-39th St. Sacramento CA 95816.

MCAFOOSE

McAfoose, Catherine (River/Shriver).

b. 1809 d. 18 May 1890 Kittaning Twp Pa.

* Researcher: Kathy Marcinek R D #6 Box 187 Kittaning PA 16201.

MEEK

Meek, Margaret.

b. Nov 27,1818 in Ill m. Aug 4, 1837 to Thomas King. d. ?

Had 10 children Adam, Amy Torre, Daniel, George, Hellen, Margaret, Mary, Nancy, Sarah, Thomas.

* Researcher: Marian R Wilder 11018 Circle "S" Rd Seffner FL 33584. 813-621-6780.

METEA

Metea.

And other Citizen or Prairie Band Potawatomi in or near Fulton County In.

* Reseacher: Fulton County Historical Society, Inc. 37 E 375 N Rochester IN 46975-8384. 219-223-4436.

MITCHELL

Mitchell, Florence.

The following has/have been located on
the Cherokee Rolls though no connection
has been made to the family.

Mitchell, family name only page 160 The
Drennen Roll Of 1852.

* Researcher: Lew Roman 277 Inverness
St Broomfield CO 80020.

Mitchell, Francis Jane.

The following has/have been located on
the Cherokee Rolls though no connection
has been made to the family.

Mitchell, family name only page 160 The
Drennen Roll Of 1852.

* Researcher: Lew Roman 277 Inverness
St Broomfield CO 80020.

Mitchell, Harry Lee.

The following has/have been located on
the Cherokee Rolls though no connection
has been made to the family.

Mitchell, family name only page 160 The
Drennen Roll Of 1852.

* Researcher: Lew Roman 277 Inverness
St Broomfield CO 80020.

Mitchell, Harry R.

The following has/have been located on
the Cherokee Rolls though no connection
has been made to the family.

Mitchell, family name only page 160 The Drennen Roll Of 1852.

* Researcher: Lew Roman 277 Inverness St Broomfield CO 80020.

Mitchell, Leona.

The following has/have been located on the Cherokee Rolls though no connection has been made to the family.

Mitchell, family name only page 160 The Drennen Roll Of 1852.

* Researcher: Lew Roman 277 Inverness St Broomfield CO 80020.

MOYE

Moye, Joe (Joseph) Jefferson.

b Apr 4, 1867 in Milltown Ga m. Mollie Cooper in Ga?

Had 5 children Hattie, Clara, John, Joe, Mary.

* Researcher: Marian R Wilder 11018 Circle "S" Rd Seffner FL 33584. 813-621-6780.

NAVARRE

Navarre, Pierre.

And other Citizen or Prairie Band Potawatomi in or near Fulton County In.

* Reseacher: Fulton County Historical Society, Inc. 37 E 375 N Rochester IN 46975-8384. 219-223-4436.

NEEDLES

Needles, John.

b. c 1640 Possibly in Piankatank River Area Va. m. c 1660 to Francis (d. 18 Nov 1697 Talbot City Md) probably in Piankatank River Area Va. # children ? John d. ? possibly in Talbot County Md near Turkey Creek.

Possibly Powhatan.

* Researcher: Jeanne L Eppley 204 Rome-Hilliard Rd Columbus Ohio 43228. 614-878-4920.

NICKOLS

Nickols, William Edward.

b.? m. c 1876 to Kate Landusky Miller in Zanesville Muskingum County Ohio d. 1926 in Zanesville Muskingum County Ohio.

Had #? children besides James.

Possibly Delaware.

* Researcher: Jeanne L Eppley 204 Rome Hilliard Rd Columbus Ohio 43228. 614-878-4920.

NIXON

Nixon, William (Brother of Sarah Nixon Smith).

b. 1824? or 1829 in SW GA or SE Al m. Sept 2 1856 to Gabriella Parr in Barbour County Al. d. June 6 1902 in Panola County Ms.

Possible Creek or Sawokli.

Had 7 children Calvin Nixon b. 1857,
Henry L. Nixon b. 1859?, Lang N Nixon b
1867, Sallie Rebecca Nixon b. 1870?,
Bertha P Nixon b. 1876, Mittie E Nixon
b. 1880, Etta Nixon d. infant.

* Researcher: Elizabeth Waldorf 2611
Parkview Dr Biloxi MS 39531-2721.

O'QUINN

O'Quinn, Tyler.

b. 1700's in Colleton County SC m. to
Elizabeth Stone in Colleton County SC
d? probably Colleton County SC.

Had an undetermined number of children
only known is a son Barry O'Quinn.

* Researcher : Sandra A Ogle 602 Pine
Forest Dr Brandon Fl 33511-7818. 813-
654-9542.

OSTANDER/OSTANDES

Ostandes, Lydia (See Lydia Adams, Lydia
Licenbegler, & Lydia Pierce.).

m. Samuel D Adams d. along with two of
her daughters in 1845 during an
outbreak of smallpox and were buried
where Union Station now stands in
Pittsburgh Pa.

* Researcher: Laurie Beth Duffy 3308
Acapulco Dr Riverview Fl 33569.

OURY

Oury, Catherine (Frantz).

61

OVERTON

Overton, David.

b. 1795 in Val NC. m. 1815 to Mary Tucker in Franlkin County Tn. d. 1874 in Shelby County AL.

Possibly Creek/Cherokee.

Had 10 children Elizabeth, Rachel, Jesse, George, Mariah, Jackson, David, Mary, William, Henry.

OWENS

Owens, Olivia.

Mother of Johnathan Edward Platts of SC, Seminole m. Adela Martin 12/20/1870 in Ga or SC. in Hall Ga census 1880 served in Civil War paroled in 1865 in Augusta Ga.

PADGETT

Padgett, Sarah.

b. 15 Feb 1865 in Kissimmee Fl Orange Co. m. 21 Aug 1881 to Charles Bass in Kissimmee Fl Rose Hille. d. 19 May 1917 Kissimmee Osceola FL Rose Hill

Cemetery.

Had 7 children Charles Bishop Jr,
Everett, Lonnie, Lottie, Mary Bell,
Verna, Willa E.

* Researcher: Marian R Wilder 11018
Circle "S" Rd Seffner FL 33584. 813-
621-6780.

PETERSON

Peterson, Elizabeth (Betsy).

b. in Ga, NC or FL m. to Needham Bass
Marriage Bond possibly Ga. d. in
Kissimmee FL Osceola Fl Rose Hill
Cemetery.

Had 9 children Betsy, Charles,
Crawford, Elvirs, Needham, Quinna,
Robinson, Robert, Selvania.

* Researcher: Marian R Wilder 11018
Circle "S" Rd Seffner FL 33584. 813-
621-6780.

PIERCE

Pierce Lydia (See Lydia Adams, Lydia
Licenbegler, Lydia Ostander, & Lydia
Ostandes.).

m. Samuel D Adams d; along with two of
her daughters in 1845 during an
outbreak of smallpox and were buried
where Union Station now stands in
Pittsburgh Pa.

* Researcher: Laurie Beth Duffy 3308
Acapulco Dr Riverview Fl 33569.

PRITCHETT

Pritchett, Croman W.

b. Aug 14, 1888 in Meecham or Mitchum Beat Alabama m? to Mary Cleveland Skipper in Lower Peachtree Al d. July 1981 of a stroke and Kidney failure in Montgomery Al.

Possibly Cherokee.

Had 5 children Lucy, Marvin, Mary Lee, S.J., Verbon.

* Researcher : Sandra A Ogle 602 Pine Forest Dr Brandon Fl 33511-7818. 813-654-9542.

RAGER

Rager, Michael.

(Brother of Margaret who married Uriah Black) b. c 1831 probably in Darke County Ohio m. Apr 26, 1854 to Susanna Wagaman in Darke County Ohio. d.?

Possibly Wyandot.

Had 2 possibly 3 children John, Mary Jane, & possibly William (who dissapeared in 1861).

* Researcher: Jeanne L Eppley 204 Rome-Hilliard Rd Columbus Ohio 43228. 614-878-4920.

RAYEN

Rayen, John.

1/4 Native American b 1792 Pa? d 1852 in Champion Oh. Black Hawk.

* Researcher: Ellen Erdman Young 630 Groveview Lane La Canada California 91011.

RAYMOND

Raymond, Amy Grace.

b. Aug 9 1875 Hillsdale Count Michigan m. Nov 3, 1889 to James Linden Ash. d. Dec 17 1923 of cancer in Detroit Michigan.

Possibly Potawatomi.

Had 6 children Margaret, Jesse, Lena, Roy, Echo, & Doris Mae.

* Researcher: Cathy May P O Box 6482 Jackson MI 49204. 517-784-8723. email TAOCAT @ AOL.

REDING

Reding, Nancy Baker.

b. 30 Sep 1818 in Davidson Co Tn m. 1834 to Andrew J Malone in Fayette Tn. d. 9 Oct 1851 in Montgomery Co TX.

Had 3 children Henderson, Thomas, William.

* Researcher: Marian R Wilder 11018 Circle "S" Rd Seffner FL 33584. 813-621-6780.

Reding, Robert.

b. 9 Oct. 1745 Redding Pasquotank NC m. 1816 to Ann Nancy Baker in Davidson Co TN.

Only known child Nancy Baker Reding. d. 11 May 1832 in Fayette CO TN.

* Researcher: Marian R Wilder 11018 Circle "S" Rd Seffner FL 33584. 813-621-6780.

ROBBINS

Robbins, William.

b. c 1817 in Pa m.? to Mary Garner in Pa or Berkley County Va. d. ? probably Delaware County Ohio.

Possibly Shawnee.

Had 12 children Nathan, John, Henry, Mary, Ellen, Charles, William, Robert, Clarinda, Diana, Amanda, Margaret (infant).

* Researcher: Jeanne L Eppley 204 Rome-Hilliard Rd Columbus Ohio 43228. 614-878-4920.

ROBERTS

Roberts, Benny.

The following has/have been located on the Cherokee Rolls though no connection has been made to the family.

Roberts, family name only page 205 The Drennen Roll Of 1852.

* Researcher: Lew Roman 277 Inverness St Broomfield CO 80020.

Roberts, Lavina (Luenna).

The following has/have been located on

the Cherokee Rolls though no connection has been made to the family.

Roberts, family name only page 205 The Drennen Roll Of 1852.

* Researcher: Lew Roman 277 Inverness St Broomfield CO 80020.

Roberts, Noah.

The following has/have been located on the Cherokee Rolls though no connection has been made to the family.

Roberts, family name only page 205 The Drennen Roll Of 1852.

* Researcher: Lew Roman 277 Inverness St Broomfield CO 80020.

Roberts, Robert.

The following has/have been located on the Cherokee Rolls though no connection has been made to the family.

Roberts, family name only page 205 The Drennen Roll Of 1852.

* Researcher: Lew Roman 277 Inverness St Broomfield CO 80020.

Roberts, Teackle.

b ? m. Nov 7, 1801 to Peggy Hutson.

Had 3 children Arthur, Rosey & Esther.

* Researcher: Sheila Carr 14912 Laurie Lane Tampa FL 33613. 813-968-9568. Pager 219-2789.

Rogers, Ed.

The following has/have been located on the Cherokee Rolls though no connection has been made to the family.

family name only page 206 The Drennen Roll Of 1852.

Rogers, Ed 11086 22835 Guion-Miller Roll Of 1909.

Rogers, Ed Jr. 4201M 22841 Guion-Miller Roll Of 1909.

* Researcher: Lew Roman 277 Inverness St Broomfield CO 80020.

Rogers, Lancyma (Luna).

* Researcher: Lew Roman 277 Inverness St Broomfield CO 80020.

Rogers, Samuel Alfred.

b ? in Michigan? m. ? to ? in ?. d. ? maybe in Michigan.

Had 4 children Alfred George, Alida, Sara, Samuel Emmanuel.

* Researcher: Marian R Wilder 11018 Circle "S" Rd Seffner FL 33584. 813-621-6780.

Rogers, Sara.

b. ? possibly Jordan Michigan m. ? to George Cooper in Jordan Michigan. d. ? in Tampa Fl.

Had 2 children Marian, Mattie.

Rogers, William Haywood.

b. ? in Raleigh NC m. 12/15/1880 to
Katie Avera Wilder in NC. d.?

Had 2 children Gaston, Katherine.

ROPER

Judy, Roper.

m. to Moxais (Muses) Hamblett.

Had 8 children Rachel Oraton, William,
James, Abner, Tans, Tillethe, Darcus,
Hanna.

Possibly Creek/Cahaba.

SHARP/SHARPE

Sharp, Susie Leona.

b. July 6, 1910 in Ruddells Mill Ky m.
Brodus Owen Hiles 22 Dec 1934 in
Covington Ky d. in Covington Ky.

The following has/have been located on
the Cherokee Rolls though no connection
has been made to the family.

Sharp family name only page 223 The
Drennen Roll Of 1852.

* Researcher: Lori Brown 6435 Green
Meadow Dr Fayettville NC 28306-5714.

SINCLAIR

Sinclair, Hugh Crige.

b. 7-13-1846 in Mississippi. m. ?
Frances Brown. d. Aug 8, 1924.

Had 8 children Annie, Emma, Eunice,
Hattey, Hector, John, Julia, Walter
Brown.

* Researcher: Marian R Wilder 11018
Circle "S" Rd Seffner FL 33584. 813-
621-6780.

SKAINS

Skains, Nancy.

b. about 1804 in SC. m. about 1820 to
Adam Skains Jr. in Sc or AL d.?

Had 11 children Adam, Charner, Francis,
James, Julia, Maria, Salina, Sarah,
Thomas, Vardell, William M.

* Researcher: Pat Talley 1574 College
Pkwy Lewisville TX 75067. email address
PLT7@aol.com. 972-436-7727.

SKIPPER

Skipper, Mary Cleveland.

b. Oct 27, 1881 in Clarke County Al m.?
to Croman W Pritchett in Lower
Peachtree AL. d. July 1961 of old age

in Montgomery AL.

Possibly Creek or Cherokee.

Had 5 children Lucy, Marvin, Mary Lee,
S.J., and Verbon.

* Researcher : Sandra A Ogle 602 Pine
Forest Dr Brandon Fl 33511-7818. 813-
654-9542.

SMITH

Smith, David "Young Eagle".

b approximately 1829. m. to Sally
Sizemore in West Virginia. d. possibly
1932.

Possibly Cherokee.

Had 2 children Thomas Hamilton, and
Maggie.

Young Eagle was nine years old when the
soldiers came to send him and his
family to join the Trail of Tears. Both
of Young Eagles parents were killed
during the march, but he survived and
escaped. He roamed the southeast until
he was found and put in an orphanage.
Young Eagle was an intelligent boy who
spoke, read and wrote the Cherokee
language, but knew nothing about the
white man.

During the next two years he learned
the language and the ways of the white
man. By this time he was too old to be
adopted and no one would have an Indian
boy; therefore he was sold into
bondage. When he was older and had
saved enough money, he bought his

freedom. He then moved on to West Virginia where he met a Cherokee girl whom he married and settled down with. He later changed his name to Thomas (should be David) Smith, after the man who had bought him from the orphanage, because he had grown to love and respect him. He and his wife Sara had two sons. One of the sons was David (should be Thomas) Smith, who was to become my Grandfather.

Young Eagle lived to the ripe old age of 103.

The Trail of Tears began the winter of 1838 and ended Spring 1839.

This story was written by my father, Douglas MacArthur Smith, in the 1950's. He appears to have switched the name of his grandfather & great-grandfather.

* Researcher: Lisa M Worley 2525-D White Oak Place Escondido Ca 92027-2865. 619-489-9350. FAX 619-571-8519.

Smith, Sara.

b. 1914 m. Arthur Sydney Baker d. 1993.

The following has/have been located on the Cherokee Rolls though no connection has been made to the family.

Smith, Sarah 1050 The Mullay Roll Of 1848.

Smith, Sara P180 The Siler Roll Of 1851.

Smith, Sara 1550 The Siler Roll Of 1851.

Smith, Sara 1357 The Siler Roll Of
1851.

Smith, family name only page 226 The
Drennen Roll Of 1852.

Smith, family name only page 227 The
Drennen Roll Of 1852.

Smith, Sarah 1303 The Swetland Roll Of
1869.

Smith, Sara U37 The Hester Roll Of
1883.

Smith, Sarah 1063 & 24978 Guion-Miller
Roll Of 1909.

Smith, Sarah 6060 & 24982 Guion-Miller
Roll Of 1909.

Smith, Sarah 15441 & 24977 Guion-Miller
Roll Of 1909.

Smith, Sarah 30686 & 24785 Guion-Miller
Roll Of 1909.

Smith, Sarah 18D Guion-Miller Roll Of
1909.

Smith, Sarah E. 21689 & 24986 Guion-
Miller Roll Of 1909.

Smith, Sarah J. 11276 & 24989 Guion-
Miller Roll Of 1909.

Smith, Sarah M. 20713 & 24972 Guion-
Miller Roll Of 1909.

Smith, Sarah P. 636 & 24991 Guion-
Miller Roll Of 1909.

* Researcher: Lew Roman 277 Inverness
St Broomfield CO 80020.

Smith, Sarah "Sally" Nixon.

(Sister of William Nixon) b 1834? SW
Ga? or SE Al. m. Jan 1847 to Andrew
Jackson Smith in Barbour County
Alabama. d. of pneumonia near Montrose
in Jasper County Ms.

Possibly Creek or Sawokli.

Had 14 children Sarah, Rebecca, Robert,
Dicy, Samantha, George, Andrew, Carey,
Emily, Aura, William, Mary, Cynthia, &
John.

* Researcher: Elizabeth Waldorf 2611
Parkview Dr Biloxi MS 39531-2721.

STALCUP

Stalcup, Elmer Ellsworth.

b 186? Lancaster County Pa m Lottie
Leona Gamble. d May 1931 buried
Arlington Cemetery Drexel Hill Pa.

* Researcher: Laurie Beth Duffy 3308
Acapulco Dr Riverview Fl 33569.

Stalcup, Florence Cordelia.

b. 8-30-1901 in Jersey Shore Pa m.
Steward Adams Whiteman 7-26-1919 at
Philadelphia Pa d. 1988.

The following has/have been located on
the Cherokee Rolls though no connection
has been made to the family.

STALCUP, Florence 22039 25332 Guion-
Miller Roll Of 1909.

* Researcher: Laurie Beth Duffy 3308

Acapulco Dr Riverview Fl 33569.

Stalcup, Lottie Leona Gamble.

b 187? Osceola Mills Clearfield County
Pa m Elmer Ellsworth Stalcup. d 1926.

* Researcher: Laurie Beth Duffy 3308
Acapulco Dr Riverview Fl 33569.

STANLEY

Stanley, Caroline.

b. 1 August 1849 in Hampton or Beaufort
County Sc. m ? to Burl Tuten in SC. d.
1892 in SC.

Had 3 known children Eliza?, Elizabeth,
and ?

* Researcher : Sandra A Ogle 602 Pine
Forest Dr Brandon Fl 33511-7818. 813-
654-9542.

SULLIVAN

Sullivan, Ellen.

b. 15 Dec 1824 m. Morgan Hiles.

* Researcher: Lori Brown 6435 Green
Meadow Dr Fayettville NC 28306-5714.

TERRELL

Terrell, Jack.

b. in Ga married to ? Carter.

Had ? children known is William Mack.

* Researcher : Marian R Wilder 11018

Circle "S" Rd Seffner FL 33584. 813-621-6780.

Terrell, William Mack.

b. in Ga.

Had one child Bearny.

Possibly Cherokee.

* Researcher : Marian R Wilder 11018 Circle "S" Rd Seffner FL 33584. 813-621-6780.

THORNTON

Thornton, Henry.

b 1860 d 1930.

The following has/have been located on the Cherokee Rolls though no connection has been made to the family.

Thornton, Henry J. 10520 26970 Guion-Miller Roll Of 1909.

* Researcher: Lew Roman 277 Inverness St Broomfield CO 80020.

TOOLE

Toole, ? Miss (first name unknown).

b. approx 1801 in Gones Co Ga m. ? to William Wilder (II).

Only known child John Andrew Jackson Wilder d. ? in Americus Ga.

* Researcher: Marian R Wilder 11018

Circle "S" Rd Seffner FL 33584. 813-621-6780.

TUCKER

Tucker, George.

b. 1744? Tn m. to Elizabeth Yahula. d. 1852 in Marion County Al.

Possibly Creek.

Had ? children Mary, Thomas, and others.

* Researcher : Nicole Sharpe Assistant Registrar Cahaba Tribal Association P O Box 51 Grandfield OK 73546-0051.

TUTEN

Tuten, Maryann Tabitha Stanley.

b. Oct 12, 1857 in Hampton or Beaufort County Sc m.? to Burl R Tuten in Hampton Co. d. Jan 16, 1888 probably in childbirth possibly in Huggins Oak Hampton County SC.

Had 2 children Cynthia and Henry.

* Researcher : Sandra A Ogle 602 Pine Forest Dr Brandon Fl 33511-7818. 813-654-9542.

VIEUX

Vieux, Louis.

And other Citizen or Prairie Band Potawatomi in or near Fulton County In.

* Reseacher: Fulton County Historical

Society, Inc. 37 E 375 N Rochester IN
46975-8384. 219-223-4436.

WABAUNSEE

Wabaunsee.

And other Citizen or Prairie Band
Potawatomi in or near Fulton County In.

* Reseacher: Fulton County Historical
Society, Inc. 37 E 375 N Rochester IN
46975-8384. 219-223-4436.

WALTERS

Walters, Mollie Ann.

b. Apr 1835 in Americus Ga m. to John
Andrew Jackson Wilder in (B) Jones Co
GA. d. 1915 in Americus Ga.

Had 3 ? children Charles, Edwin,
Linton.

* Researcher: Marian R Wilder 11018
Circle "S" Rd Seffner FL 33584. 813-
621-6780.

WAMEGO

Wamego.

And other Citizen or Prairie Band
Potawatomi in or near Fulton County In.

* Reseacher: Fulton County Historical
Society, Inc. 37 E 375 N Rochester IN
46975-8384. 219-223-4436.

WHITE

White, Benjamin.

The following has/have been located on the Cherokee Rolls though no connection has been made to the family.

White, family name only page 235 The Drennen Roll Of 1852.

* Researcher: Lew Roman 277 Inverness St Broomfield CO 80020.

White, Eleanore Joy.

The following has/have been located on the Cherokee Rolls though no connection has been made to the family.

White, family name only page 235 The Drennen Roll Of 1852.

* Researcher: Lew Roman 277 Inverness St Broomfield CO 80020.

White, Elizabeth.

The following has/have been located on the Cherokee Rolls though no connection has been made to the family.

White, Elizabeth Family G 58 The Old Settler Roll Of 1851.

White, family name only page 235 The Drennen Roll Of 1852.

* Researcher: Lew Roman 277 Inverness St Broomfield CO 80020.

White, Eva (Retta?).

The following has/have been located on the Cherokee Rolls though no connection has been made to the family.

White, Eva M. 29010 Guion-Miller Roll Of 1909.

White, Eva Maloy 3648M Guion-Miller Roll Of 1909.

White, family name only page 235 The Drennen Roll Of 1852.

* Researcher: Lew Roman 277 Inverness St Broomfield CO 80020.

White, Fisher.

The following has/have been located on the Cherokee Rolls though no connection has been made to the family.

White, family name only page 235 The Drennen Roll Of 1852.

* Researcher: Lew Roman 277 Inverness St Broomfield CO 80020.

White, Garnet.

The following has/have been located on the Cherokee Rolls though no connection has been made to the family.

White, family name only page 235 The Drennen Roll Of 1852.

* Researcher: Lew Roman 277 Inverness St Broomfield CO 80020.

White, George.

The following has/have been located on the Cherokee Rolls though no connection has been made to the family.

White, George Family G 37 The Old

Settler Roll Of 1851.

White, George 1809 29004 Guion-Miller Roll Of 1909.

White, George 18633 Guion-Miller Roll Of 1909.

White, George 1038M Guion-Miller Roll Of 1909.

White, George W. 21574 Guion-Miller Roll Of 1909.

White, family name only page 235 The Drennen Roll Of 1852.

* Researcher: Lew Roman 277 Inverness St Broomfield CO 80020.

White, Hannah.

The following has/have been located on the Cherokee Rolls though no connection has been made to the family.

White, family name only page 235 The Drennen Roll Of 1852.

* Researcher: Lew Roman 277 Inverness St Broomfield CO 80020.

White, Harriet.

The following has/have been located on the Cherokee Rolls though no connection has been made to the family.

White, family name only page 235 The Drennn Roll Of 1852.

* Researcher: Lew Roman 277 Inverness St Broomfield CO 80020.

White, Harry.

The following has/have been located on the Cherokee Rolls though no connection has been made to the family.

White, family name only page 235 The Drennen Roll Of 1852.

* Researcher: Lew Roman 277 Inverness St Broomfield CO 80020.

White, James.

The following has/have been located on the Cherokee Rolls though no connection has been made to the family.

White, James 1804 28999 Guion-Miller Roll Of 1909.

White, James 17714 15171 Guion-Miller Roll Of 1909.

White, James A. 21572 Guion-Miller Roll Of 1909.

White, family name only page 235 The Drennen Roll Of 1852.

* Researcher: Lew Roman 277 Inverness St Broomfield CO 80020.

White, John.

The following has/have been located on the Cherokee Rolls though no connection has been made to the family.

White, John 2998 The Baker Roll Of 1924.

White, John Family G 58 The Old Settler

Roll Of 1851.

White, family name only page 235 The
Drennen Roll Of 1852.

* Researcher: Lew Roman 277 Inverness
St Broomfield CO 80020.

White, Joseph.

The following has/have been located on
the Cherokee Rolls though no connection
has been made to the family.

White, Joseph 13563 Guion-Miller Roll
Of 1909.

White, family name only page 235 The
Drennen Roll Of 1852.

* Researcher: Lew Roman 277 Inverness
St Broomfield CO 80020.

White, Lawn Ellis.

The following has/have been located on
the Cherokee Rolls though no connection
has been made to the family.

White, family name only page 235 The
Drennen Roll Of 1852.

* Researcher: Lew Roman 277 Inverness
St Broomfield CO 80020.

White, Mary.

The following has/have been located on
the Cherokee Rolls though no connection
has been made to the family.

White, Mary (May) 2996 The Baker Roll
Of 1924.

White, Mary Family G 58 The Old Settler
Roll Of 1851.

White, Mary 17767 29011 Guion-Miller
Roll Of 1909.

White, Mary 21561 Guion-Miller Roll Of
1909.

White, Mary 46D Guion-Miller Roll Of
1909.

White, Mary 47D Guion-Miller Roll Of
1909.

White, Mary M. 11098 29014 Guion-Miller
Roll Of 1909.

White, Mary P. 21563 Guion-Miller Roll
Of 1909.

White, family name only page 235 The
Drennen Roll Of 1852.

* Researcher: Lew Roman 277 Inverness
St Broomfield CO 80020.

White, Matilda.

The following has/have been located on
the Cherokee Rolls though no connection
has been made to the family.

White, family name only page 235 The
Drennen Roll Of 1852.

* Researcher: Lew Roman 277 Inverness
St Broomfield CO 80020.

White, Otto.

The following has/have been located on
the Cherokee Rolls though no connection
has been made to the family.

White, Otto 1014M Guion-Miller Roll Of 1909.

White, family name only page 235 The Drennen Roll Of 1852.

* Researcher: Lew Roman 277 Inverness St Broomfield CO 80020.

White, Rebecca Ann.

The following has/have been located on the Cherokee Rolls though no connection has been made to the family.

White, family name only page 235 The Drennen Roll Of 1852.

* Researcher: Lew Roman 277 Inverness St Broomfield CO 80020.

White, Samuel.

The following has/have been located on the Cherokee Rolls though no connection has been made to the family.

White, Samuel 31258 Guion-Miller Roll Of 1909.

White, family name only page 235 The Drennen Roll Of 1852.

* Researcher: Lew Roman 277 Inverness St Broomfield CO 80020.

White, Sarah.

The following has/have been located on the Cherokee Rolls though no connection has been made to the family.

White, Sarah Family G 58 The Old

Settler Roll Of 1851.

White, Sarah M. 29021 Guion-Miller Roll Of 1909.

White, Sarah M. 29426 Guion-Miller Roll Of 1909.

White, family name only page 235 The Drennen Roll Of 1852.

* Researcher: Lew Roman 277 Inverness St Broomfield CO 80020.

White, Wesley.

The following has/have been located on the Cherokee Rolls though no connection has been made to the family.

White, family name only page 235 The Drennen Roll Of 1852.

* Researcher: Lew Roman 277 Inverness St Broomfield CO 80020.

White, William.

The following has/have been located on the Cherokee Rolls though no connection has been made to the family.

White, William 92D Guion-Miller Roll Of 1909.

White, William J. 21564 Guion-Miller Roll Of 1909.

White, Willie G. 21564 Guion-Miller Roll Of 1909.

White, family name only page 235 The Drennen Roll Of 1852.

White, William H.

The following has/have been located on
the Cherokee Rolls though no connection
has been made to the family.

White, William 92D Guion-Miller Roll Of
1909.

White, William J. 21564 Guion-Miller
Roll Of 1909.

White, family name only page 235 The
Drennen Roll Of 1852.

WILCOX

Wilcox, Ann.

The following has/have been located on
the Cherokee Rolls though no connection
has been made to the family.

Wilcox, family name only page 236 The
Drennen Roll Of 1852

Wilcox, Carol.

The following has/have been located on
the Cherokee Rolls though no connection
has been made to the family.

Wilcox, family name only page 236 The
Drennen Roll Of 1852.

* Researcher: Lew Roman 277 Inverness
St Broomfield CO 80020.

Wilcox, Gayle.

The following has/have been located on
the Cherokee Rolls though no connection
has been made to the family.

Wilcox, family name only page 236 The
Drennen Roll Of 1852.

* Researcher: Lew Roman 277 Inverness
St Broomfield CO 80020.

Wilcox, Stephen.

The following has/have been located on
the Cherokee Rolls though no connection
has been made to the family.

Wilcox, family name only page 236 The
Drennen Roll Of 1852.

* Researcher: Lew Roman 277 Inverness
St Broomfield CO 80020.

Wilcox, Sue.

The following has/have been located on
the Cherokee Rolls though no connection
has been made to the family.

Wilcox, family name only page 236 The
Drennen Roll Of 1852.

* Researcher: Lew Roman 277 Inverness
St Broomfield CO 80020.

WILDER

Wilder, Willis.

b. 6/10/1755 in Tar River Nc Edgecombe Co m. to ?

Only known child William Wilder (II) d. 1835 in Jones Co Ga.

* Researcher: Marian R Wilder 11018 Circle "S" Rd Seffner FL 33584. 813-621-6780.

WILKENSON

Wilkenson, Harriet Moss (Moss was the Indian name).

b? m ? to T J Gibson in TX d? in Texas Possible Tribal affiliation Cherokee.

Had one known child Sarah Ann Elizea in 1853.

* Researcher: Pat Talley 1574 College Pkwy Lewisville TX 75067 email address PLT7@aol.com. 972-436-7727.

WILLIAMS

Williams, Nancy.

The following has/have been located on the Cherokee Rolls though no connection has been made to the family.

Williams, Nancy 14302 Dawes# Miller#.

Williams, Nancy 5334 Dawes# Miller#.

Williams, Nancy E Family G 10 The Old Settler Roll Of 1851.

Williams, family name only page 238 The Drennen Roll Of 1852.

* Researcher: Lori Brown 6435 Green Meadow Dr Fayettville NC 28306-5714.

WILLIS

Willis, Kathryn.

The following has/have been located on the Cherokee Rolls though no connection has been made to the family.

Willis, Catherine #2007 The Siler Roll Of 1851.

Willis, family name only page 238 The Drennen Roll Of 1852.

* Researcher: Lew Roman 277 Inverness St Broomfield CO 80020.

WILSON

Wilson, Benjamin Franklin.

b. Mar 27 1853 b. 1880 ? 2nd wife Louise (Lou) C Gidings. d. 1918 of Rattle Snake Bite in Terry Town, Webster or Linden Fl.

Possibly Cherokee or Creek.

Had 1 son with first wife, 12 children with 2nd. Charlie, Josephine, Beula (Giddeons), Ella (Tillus or Merritt), Mamie, Gena (Merritt), Matilda (Whitman), Benjamin, Franklin, Carrie (Langston), George, Missouri (Zury) (Merritt, McCrone), Wynn, Minnie Mae (Rogers).

Family oral History says he came from Oklahoma in a covered wagon.

WOODRUFF

Woodruff, Joshua.

b. c 1797 in Greene County Pa m.? to
Priscilla Davis. d.? in Knox of Licking
County Ohio.

Possibly Shawnee.

Had 11 children Mary, Benjamin, James,
David, Amanda, Vasti, Maria, Calvin,
Louis, Joshua, Morgan.

WRIGHT

Wright, Clarisa.

The following has/have been located on
the Cherokee Rolls though no connection
has been made to the family.

Wright, family name only page 243 The
Drennen Roll Of 1852.

Wright, Eunice.

The following has/have been located on
the Cherokee Rolls though no connection
has been made to the family.

Wright, family name only page 243 The

Drennen Roll Of 1852.

* Researcher: Lew Roman 277 Inverness St Broomfield CO 80020.

YAHULA

Yahula, Elizabeth.

b. 1780's in TN m. George Tucker. d. 1821.

Possibly Creek.

Had ? children Thomas, Mary.

* Researcher : Nicole Sharpe Assistant Registrar Cahaba Tribal Association P O Box 51 Grandfield OK 73546-0051.

ZERRY

Zerry, Thomas.

b. 1772 in Ga? m. Jonanen X (Full Blood Creek) in Ga? d. 1816 Morgan County Ga.

Possibly Creek.

Had 9 children Sarah, William, Tom, Nancy, Emily, Nellie, John, Mary, Elizabeth.

* Researcher : Nicole Sharpe Assistant Registrar Cahaba Tribal Association P O Box 51 Grandfield OK 73546-0051.

SECTION II

INDIAN TRIBES AND ORGANIZATIONS
SEARCHING FOR LOST TRIBAL MEMBERS

Many of the addresses in this section were provided by Chief Piercing Eyes Penn of the Pan American Indian Association Inc, their lists are updated daily with Groups, Tribes, Chiefs, Teachers & Active Participants in Revival. They invite additions and corrections from readers. A complete updated list is available for $20.00, partial lists by state or Tribe $4.00 from the Pan American Indian Association Inc. Archives Library Nocatee Fl 34268-0244 (941) 494-6930.

Pan American Indian Association a non profit organization with over 3,700 members. Publishes a monthly newspaper called the Earth Keeper. Principal Chief, Editor & Publisher Thom "Raven Hawk" Sturgill Pan American Indians POB 56, Murphy NC 28906.

Big Horn Lenape Federation and the Lenape of Ohio Wolf Band Church. A non profit organization not affiliated with any other Lenape group. They welcome others to come and visit and see what they are all about. This contact was from Horse Woman Nahni one gus X kue Wolf Clan Mother and Meteinu of the Church. 1056 West Rd Martinsville Ohio 45146-9551.

Cahaba Tribal Association Inc descendants of one of the Cahaba Tribes from the homelands of Alabama. Creek, Choctaws, Cherokee, Chickasawa, Hillabee and other tribes whose names are lost in the wind. Nicki Sharpe Assistant Registrar PO Box 51 Grandfield OK 73546-0051. email CAHABA CREEKS at JUNO @.COM.

The Free Cherokee Confederation members in TN; GA; AL; MO; OK; TX; & VA. people of Cherokee descent and their families. Proof of descent shall include notarized affidavits of personal knowledge, family Bible or family records. In the interest of the Band strength and integrity, affidavits shall be required. Principal Chief Robert T Murray 604 Ridgeland Rd Rossville Ga 30741 (706) 820-0458.

Nacion Taina, Robinson Urayoan Rosado, Nitayno, Residencial Jaguas #C5, Clales

PR 00638 (809) 871-3012. Has a bilingual newsletter.

(Taino) Caney 5th World Learning Lodge, Grandmother Maniki Guarichegua Cemi, HC 01 Box 5761, Clales PR 00638-9624 (809) 376- 0494 (Celular Phone).

Nacion Taina, Chief Rene Cibanacan, POB 1126, Trujillo Alto PR 00977-1126 (809) 760-6218.

Free Cherokees, Wild Potato Band, Chief Rainbow Newmoon Shootingstar, POB 385, Feeding Hill MA 01030-0385 (413) 785- 5912 Publishes the Free Cherokee Newsletter.

Red Tail Alliance, Chief O'Tee, Ray Gauthier POB 466 Garnder Ma 01440-0466.

Nipmuc Tribe, Hassanamisco Band, Chief Walter Vickers 2 Longfellow Rd Northborough MA 01532 (617) 943-4569.

The Free Cherokees, Eagle Council Chief Wounded Eagle 21 Shackford Rd Reading MA 01867 (617) 944-3243.

New England Coastal Shaghticoke Indian Association & Tribal Council POB 551 Avon MA 02322-0551.

Mashpee Wampanoag Indian Tribal Council Chief Russell Peters 89 Shellback Way #N Mashpee MA 02649-3302 (617) 477-1825 publish a quarterly Nashauonk Mittark.

Penobscot Tribe Community Bldg Indian Island Old Town ME 04468 (207) 827-7776 FAX (207) 827-6042.

Pleasant Point Passamaquoddy Rez. POB 343 Perry ME 04667-0343 (207) 853-2600

FAX (207) 853-6039.

Indian Township Passamaquoddy Rez POB 301 Princeton ME 04668-0301 (207) 796-2301 FAX (207) 796-5256.

Houlton Band of Maliseet Indians Rt 3_box 450 Houlton ME 04730-9514 (207) 532-4273 FAX (207) 532-2660.

Aroostook Band of Mic Macs POB 772 Presque Isle ME 04769 (207) 622-4731 FAX (207) 764-7667.

The Free Cherokee Tribal Council Chief Distant Eagle 77 Main St Springfield VT 05156 Work (802) 885-5728 Home (802) 886-8452.

Green Mountain Band of Cherokee Evlyn & Kenneth Dubar 91 North F Street Bristol VT 05443 (802) 453-2750.

Vermont Abenakis St Francis/Sokoi Band Chief Homer St Francis POB 276 Swanton VT 05488-0276 (802) 868-2559.

Bear Tribe Contact Karl E Slick @ Sage Mountain POB 420 E Barre VT 05649-0420 (401) 885-4296.

Paucatuck Pequot Tribe Chief Agnes Cunha 939 Latern Hill Rd Ledyard CT 06339 (203) 572-9899.

Mohegan Tribe Chief Ralph Sturgis 27 Church Lane Uncasville CT 06382 (203) 442-8005.

Golden Hill Paugessett Tribe Chief Aurelius Piper POB 120 Trumbill CT 06611-0120 (203) 377-4410.

Bear Tribe Contact Starhawk McDonald 16

Bell Rd Cornwall Bridge CT 06754 (203) 672-3313.

Shaghticoke Indian Tribe Chief Richard Velkey 626 Washington Rd Woodbury CT 06798 (203) 263-0439.

Pan-Am Indians Weequahic Band LaVern "Shadow Ghost" Alston POB 386 East Orange NJ 07019 Home (201) 672-1978 Work (201) 648-4235.

Native Delaware Indian New Jersey Indian Office 300 Main St #3F Orange NJ 07050 (201) 675-0694.

Pan-Am Indians Weequahic Band Chief Curtis "Brown Hawk" Bey POB 1855 Newark NJ 07101-1855 (201) 622-6314.

Ramapough (Ramapo?) Mountain Indians Chief Ronald Van Dunk POB 478 Mahwah NJ 07430-0478 (201) 529-5750.

Powhattan Lenape Nation POB 225 Rancocas NJ 08073-0225 (609) 261-4747.

Nanticoke Lenni-Lenape Indians Chairman Mark M Gould 18 E Commerce St Bridgeton NJ 08302 (606) 455-0821/6910.

The Free Cherokees osprey Band Chief Medicine Hawk POB 673 Mays Landing NJ 08330 (609) 625-4129.

Taino Intertribal Council Inc Pres Peter Guanikeyu 527 Mulberry St Millville NJ 08332 (609) 825-7776/News service -7922.

Nacion Taina Chief Rene Cibanacan POB 883 NY NY 10025-0883 (212) 866-4573.

NorthEastern Native American

Association Chief William "Wassaja" Gibson 198-04 120th Ave St Albans NY 11412 (718) 978-7057.

The Free Cherokees Eagle Der Band Chief Black Eagle 146-16 220th St Rosedale Queens NY 11413 (718) 723-0921.

Northeastern Native American Association Pat "Free Spirit" Moore POB 266 Jamaica NY 11423-0266 (718) 297-6464.

Northeastern Native American Association CM Tena "Whispering Leaves" Powell 114-12 175th St St Albans NY 11434 (718) 297-7632.

Poospatuck Tribe & Reservation Chief Howard E Treadwell 198 Poospatuck Lane Mastic NY 11950 (516) 399-3843.

Southeastern Cherokee Confederacy Marshall Samuel Beler Jr WESA 36 Overlook Cr Mastic NY 11950-4913 (516) 281-6343.

Montauk Indian Tribe Hempstead Drive Sag Harbor NY 11963.

Shinnecock Tribe Trustee Brad Smith POB 59 Southhampton NY 11968-0059 (516) 283-1643.

Bear Tribe Contact Vicki Koenig & Rick Alfandre 128 Reston Rd Highland NY 12528 (914) 255-2398.

The Free Cherokees Marcia Boling Rt 1 Box 4 North Hudson NY 12855-9801 (518) 532-0570.

The Free Cherokees Many Walks Council Chief Blue Flame Moon POB 54 Stony

Creek NY 12878-0054 (518) 696-3180 publishes Fireweed.

Bear Tribe Contact Joseph Seftel 23 Denton Rd Schuyler Falls NY 12985 (518) 643-8508.

Otsiningo Iroquois Studies Association 28 Zevan Rd Johnson City NY 13790.

The Free Cherokees Wolf Council Chief Karen Thomas 3414 Heather Brook Lane Macedon NY 14502 last (716) 889-7272.

Moonrainbow 46 Finch St Rochester NY 14613 (716) 647-1532.

Big Horn Lenape Nation Chief James Hitakonanulaxk "Treebeard" Chamberlain Box 73 Chemung NY 14825-0073 (607) 3527.

Big Horn Lenape Nation Chief Xinkwemaxkwe "Big Bear" Johnson 81 Stermer Rd Elmire NY 14901-9230.

Cherokee of Virginia D Michael Wolfe 4167 Timberline Dr Allison Park PA 15101 (412) 487-7093.

Dellah White Cloud United Cherokee of WV & KY 123 Turkeyfoot Rd Sewickly PA 15143 Principle Chief Brnard Humbles-Penn (412) 741-8176.

Council of the Three Rivers American Indian Center Inc 200 Charles St Pittsburgh Pa 15238 (412) 782-4457 FAX (412) 767-4808.

Cherokee Unity Council Alice Langtry 418 Manordale Rd Pittsburgh Pa 15421.

LOST/League of Separated tribes Pat
Sellinger POB 68 Saltsburg PA 15681-
0068 publishes "Native Drums".

Native American Indian Community Brandy
Weesayha Myers Rt 2-Box 247-A Kittaning
P 16201 (412) 548-7335.

People of Earth 13439 Lovell Rd Corry
Pa 16407.

Big Horn Lenape Nation Chief
Tamakwanaxk "Beaver" Hodge Rt 3 Box
240A Gillet Pa 16915.

Mingo Tribe Chief Jerry "Talking Bear"
Dietz Box 99 Walnut Valley Farm
Loganville Pa 17342-5099.

Bear Tribe Contact Dixie Carlson Wind
Daughter West Winds Rt 5 Box 478
Bloomsburg Pa 17815 (717) 387-8659.

Blue Mountain Band of Lunapahocking
Chief Tom Big warrior POB 4362
Allentown Pa 18105-4362.

United Eastern Munsee Band Chief Dan
Bear Claw Rt 1 Box 1129 Forksville Pa
18616.

Lenape Homeland Band Chief William S
Bock 252 E Summit St Souderton PA
18964.

United Eastern Lenape Band Chief James
"Brant" Harmony HSL-94 NAS Willow Grove
PA 19090.

The Bear Tribe East Coast Office
Director WabunWind POB 199 Devon PA
19333-0199 (215) 993-3344 FAX(215) 993-
3345.

Bear Tribe Contact Sara Sheehan 7 Frazier Ave Malvern PA 19355 (610) 647-0958.

United Eastern Lenape Band Chief Bob" Red Hawk" Ruth 81 E Main St Norriston PA 19401.

Nanticoke Tribe Chief Kenneth Clark RD 4 Box 107-A Millsboro DE 19966 (302) 945-3400.

Seminole Nation Of Florida Contact Robert Coulter Indian Law Center 601 E St SE Washington DC 20003 (202) 547-2800.

Piscataway Indian Tribe Maryland Indian Heritage Society P{OB 905 Waldorf MD 20601-0905.

The Free Cherokees Tribal Agent Gentle Spirit Box 414 Chaptico MD 20621-0414 (301) 884-0143 Publishes the New Phoenix $15.00 quarterly.

The Free Cherokees Wild Potato Band Council Chair Chief Clay Basket 577 Joy Lane Hollywood MD 20636 (301) 373-8584.

The Free Cherokees Grandfather Chief Sing Alone Duncan 800 Oak Dr. Mechanicville MD 20659 (301) 884-5605.

Cherokees of Virginia Chief SW Beeler Sr 11293 Wilhoite Lane Rapidan VA 22733-2327 (703) 487-5116.

United Rappahannock Tribe Chief Alvin Winston Indian Neck VA 23077 (804) 769-3128.

Chickahominy Tribe Chief Adkins 6801 S Lott Carey Providence Forge VA 23104

(804) 829-2186.

The Free Cherokees Spider Clan Ann Walking Bear Seay POB 11472 Richmond VA 23230-1472 (804) Hone 358-8345/Work 355-0529.

Ani-Stahini/Unami Nation Harry Dyer 206 I Jefferies Drive Radford VA 24141.

Ani-Stahini/Unami Nation Eric W Miller 130 10 St NW #10 Pulaski VA 24301.

Ani-Stahini/Unami Nation Misty Dawn Thomas/Shintuck Grey Eagle Rt 1 Box 335 Ivanhoe VA 24350 (703) 744-3640.

Bear Tribe Contact Laura Weaver Center of Truth & Vision POB 777 Churchville VA 24421-0777 (703) 337-7240.

Turtle Band of Cherokee Chief Perry "Gray Wolf" Wilson Rt 3 Box 194 Evington VA 24550 (804) 525-4271.

United Cherokee Tribe of VA POB 1104 Madison Heights VA 24572 (804) 845-5606.

Seneca Indian Historical Society Wolf Spring Song Rt 1 Box 357 Wingina VA 24599 (804) 933-4399.

Northern Tsalagi Indian Tribe of SW Virginia 1813 Chandler St Burlington NC 27217-8706 Chief Vivian "Gentle Bear" Santini (919) 584-4834/5834?.

Southeastern Cherokee Confederacy Secretary Sara "Falling Star" Russell 9114 NC 49 North Cedar Grove NC 27231 (919) 562-4222.

Southeastern Cherokee Confederacy

Alternate Directory Terry "Shadow Walker" Riggins 108 Third St Haw River NC 27258 (919) 562-0995.

Eno-Occanneechi Tribe Assistant Chief John "Blackfeather" Jeffries RT 2 Box 383 Mebane NC 27302 (919) 563-4640.

Person County Indians Rt 6 Box 104 Roxboro NC 27572.

Cherokee-Powhattan Association Contact Ms Dorothy Crowe POB 3265 Roxboro NC 27573-3265 (919) 599-6448.

Haliwa-Saponi Indian Tribe Chief W R Richardson POB 99 Hollister NC 27844-0099 (919) 586-4017.

Meherrin Indian Tribe Chief George Earl Pierce POB 508 Winton NC 27986-0508 (919) 358-4375.

Cherokee Unity Council David & Barbara Krusen 2617 Meadowlark Lane Gastonia NC 28056 (704) 824-3282.

Metrolina Native American Association Robin Strickland 2601 E 7th St Charlotte NC 28204 (704) 331-4818.

Hattadare Indian Nation Chief James "Little Beaver" Lowery Sr Rt 1 Box 85-B Bunnlevel NC 28323 (919) 893-2512.

Cohairie Intertribal Council Chief Ronnie Simmons Rt 3 Box 356-B Clinton NC 28328.

Cherokee Indians of Hoke City Chief Edgar Bryant Rt 1 Box 129-C Lumber Bridge NC 28357 (919) 975-0222.

Hattaras Tuscarora Indian Tribe Chief

Vernon Locklear RT 4 Box 61 Maxton NC
28364 (919) 521-2426.

Tuscarora Nation of N Carolina Chief
Leon Locklear Rt 4 Box 172 Maxton NC
28364 (919) 844-3352.

Eastern Tuscarora Chief Keefer Locklear
POB 565 Pembroke NC 28372 (919) 521-
2655.

Lumbee Regional Association Chief
Roderick Locklear POB 68 Pembroke NC
28372-0068 (919) 521-2401 FAX (919)
521-8625.

Cherokee Tribe of Robeson County Rt 2
Box 272-A Red Springs NC 28377.

Waccamaw Siouan Tribe Chief Ervin
Jacobs POB 221 Bolton NC 28423-0221
(919) 655-8778.

Corre (Faircloth) Indian Tribe Chief
Jerry Faircloth 111 Neal Dr Atlantic NC
28511 (919) 225-0164.

Pine Tree Clan of Creek-Cherokee
Indians Chief Thelma "Fire Eyes"
Stevenson POB 110 Cherokee NC 28719-
0110.

Bear Tribe Contact Page Bryant Guynup
707 Brunswick Drive Waynesville NC
28786 (704) 456-6714.

Santee Tribe White Oak Indian Community
Chief Melvin Jackson RT 1 Box 34-M
Holly Hill SC 29059.

Bear Tribe Contact Kenneth Trogdon PhD
1921-A Pickens St Columbia SC 29201
(803) 799-6474 FAX (803) 256-4242.

Free Cherokee/Chickamauga Steven W Lux 725 Cliffside Highway Chesnee SC 29323.

Four Holes Indian Organization Edisto/Natchez/Kusso Tribe 1125 Ridge Road Ridgeville SC 29472 Chief Herb McAmis (803) 871-2126.

Chicora-Siouan Indian People Chief Gene Martin Rt 1 Box 212-M Andrews SC 29510-9801.

Pee Dee Indian Association POB 6068 Clio SC 29525-6068.

Catawba Indian Tribe POB 11106 Rock Hill SC 29730-1106 (803) 366-4792 FAX (803) 366-9150.

Free Cherokee-Turtle Clan Michael Ellison 600 Lions Club Dr Mableton GA 30059 (404) 739-5822.

Free Cherokee Good Medicine Society Steve "Rainbow Walker" Schiavl 591 Elizabeth Lane Mableton GA 30059 (404) 948-4562.

Free Cherokee TurtleClan Talking Stick Carrier Gary "Night Owl" Smith POB 672168 Marietta GA 3006702168 (404) 528-9197.

Cherokees of Georgia Chief George Hegstrom & Hon Jun Hegstron 3291 Church St Scottsdale GA 30079 (404) 299-2940 FAX (404) 294-5313.

The Free Cherokees Turtle Clan Chief Swift Hawk 235 Cherokee Village Dr Ball Ground GA 30107 (706) 735-4197.

The Free Cherokees Good Medicine

Society Director Lamar Sneed 2170
Poplar Trail Cumming GA 30131-4894.

United Eastern Lenape Band Chief James
Baxter 927 Gunter Circle Lawrenceville
GA 30243.

Cherokee Nation of Texas Charles
Thurmond Tsali Standginbear POB 1324
Clayton GA 3330525-1324 (706) 746-2448.

Cane Break Band of Eastern Cherokees
Chief Mary Cain Rt 3 Box 750 Dahlonega
GA 30533 (404) 864-6018.

Georgia Tribe of Eastern Cherokees
Chief Thomas Mote RT 3 Box 3162
Dawsonville GA 30534 (404) 427-8299.

Wolf Clan KBTI Blythe Publishing Donn F
Blythe 13578 West Highway 136 Rising
Fawn GA 30738 (706) 398-8738.

Wolf Clan KBTI Chief Dan "Lone Wolf"
Blevins Rt 1 Box 107-B Rising Fawn GA
30738 (706) 462-2531.

Wolf Clan KBTI Pat & Bill "White Wolf"
Blevins 13578 West Highway 136 Rising
Fawn GA 30738 (706) 398-0832.

Cherokee Unity Council Deloria B Harris
Rt 1 Box 107-B Rising Fawn GA 30738
(706) 462-2312.

Cherokee Unity Council Laela Sema 728
Indian Ave Rossville GA 30741.

Cherokee Unity Council Michail Redhawk
Keeper of the Wind 1831 Everglades Blvd
Rossville GA 30741.

Chickamauga Cherokee Band of NW GA

Chief Bob "Silver Fox" Murray 604
Ridgeland RD Rossville GA 30741-6103
(706) 820-0456.

Cherokee Unity Council Melton E Scott
Rt 2 Box 202-D Trenton GA 30752.

Cherokee Unity Council Ronnie "War
Eagle " Wilson 2248 Leeway Dr Augusta
GA 30903 (706) 733-2997.

Bear Clan Amonsoquath Tribe Deputy
Chief Lora Wall 114 Pechtree Blvd
Noaire GA 31005.

The Badger Council Chief Little Wolf
Lange 152 Scrubby Bluff Rd Lot 183
Kingsland GA 31547-9112.

Southeastern Cherokee Confederacy
Historian "White Wolf" Crider 318
Crestview DR Valdoast GA 31602 (912)
244-9104.

Southeastern Cherokee Confederacy Elder
John "wind Eagle" Oliver 2230 Oak Grove
Circle Valdosta GA 31602-2203.

Southeastern Cherokee Confederacy Bear
Clan Chief Sam "Sundown" Felts RT 3 Box
291 Adel GA 31620 (912) 896-3112.

Southeastern Cherokee Confederacy
Treasurer Randly "Shiled Wolf"
Christian 3895 Shelton Rd Lake Park GA
31636 (912) 242-3504.

Southeastern Cherokee Confederacy Velma
"Little Sparrow" Sublett POB 85 Lake
Park GA 31636-0085 (912) 559-4281 FAX -
1500 Editor Cherokee Talking Leaves.

Cherokee Indians Of Georgia Chief James

Young Bear 1809 Fulton Ave Albany Ga
31705 (912) 436-1605.

American Cherokee Confederacy Chief
Rattlesnake Jackson Rt 4 Box 120 Albany
GA 31705 (912) 787-5722.

Southeastern Cherokee Confederacy
Principle Chief Vivian "Panther" Lawson
POB 367 Ochlocknee GA 31773-0367 (912)
574-5497.

Southeastern Cherokee Confederacy
Director Robert "Gator" Eubanks 1448
Minton RD Sylvester GA 31791 (912) 776-
7538.

Deer Clan of SE Cherokee Confederacy
Chief Raymond "Grey Wolf" Lawson POB
1784 Thomasville GA 31799-1784 (912)
574-2953.

Cherokees of Georgia Annette Jourdan RT
2 Box 394J Hilliard FL 32046 (904) 269-
8865.

Cherokees of Georgia Chief C Jerry
"Lone Oak" Martin Rt 1 Box 906
Sanderson FL 32087.

Ocklevhua Band os Seminole-Yamasee
Principle Chief Running Buck Buford POB
521 Orange Springs FL 32182-0521 (904)
546-1386.

Apalachicola Creek Indians Blount Band
Chairwoman Mary Blount 104 W 4th Ave
Tallahassee Fl 32301 (904) 222-4538.

Topachula Indian Community Pine Arbor
Tribal Town POB 2127 Tallahassee Fl
32316-2127.

Shawnee Indians Chief Tall Bear POB 964 Crawforville FL 32326-0964.

Muskogee Creek Nation Ancilla Clan David Medicine Red Eagle Maddos Rt 5 Box 423 Perry Fl 32347.

Choctawhatchee Lower Muskogee Indians of Florida Chief "Red Eagle" Hood 6944 Cox Rd Bascom FL 32423-9406 (904) 592-4401.

Bear Clan Amonsoquath Tribe Judge Bud Alford Rt 5 Box 78X-7 DeFuniak Springs Fl 32433.

Bear Clan Amonsoquath Tribe of Cherokee Gail "Water Woman" Alford 169 Imperial Court DeFuniak Springs Fl 32433 (904) 892-4842.

Amonsoquath Tribe of Cherokee Bear Clan 5 N 24th St Defuniak Springs FL 32433 Chief Sally Time Walker Blackwell Phone & FAX (904) 892-5870.

North Bay Clan of Lower Creeks Chief Lonzo Woods POB 687 Lynn Haven FL 32444-0067.

Fading Trail Clan Chief Wilbert "Fish Eagle" Evans POB No1 Point Washington FL 32454-0001 (904) 231-4324.

Florida Tribe of Eastern Creeks Chief Donald Sharon POB 28 Bruce FL 32455-0028 (904) 835-2078.

E-Chota Cherokee Tribe of Florida Principle Chief Sally Joe Amason POB 325 Sneads Fl 32460-0325 (904) 593-5176.

Santa Rosa County Creek Indians Chief
Tom Nichols 4344 US Hwy 90 #A Pace FL
32571 Chief Nichols (904) 994-4882
Bobby Tyree (904) 623-2903.

Santa Rosa County Clan of Creek Indians
c/o Council Person Francis H Elliot POB
3486 Milton FL 32572-3486 (904) 623-
2525.

The Free Cherokees National Veterans
Band Chief Lone Wolf Howell POB 801
DeLand Fl 32721-0801 (904) 736-8050.

Tuscola United Cherokee Tribe Chief
Rhoden POB S Geneva FL 32732-0005 (407)
349-5257.

Bear Tribe Contact Elizabeth Cruz 3122
Amherst Ave Orlando Fl 32804 (407) 426-
8812.

SE Cherokee Confederacy Chief Cleve
"Light Foot" Brown 5452 N Dean Rd
Orlando FL 32817 (407) 657-0704.

Cherokee Croatan-Tchalaki Clanmother
Edith "Leaping Deer" Rains 770 NE 147th
St N Miami Fl 33161 (305) 947-4713.

Seneca Wolf Clan Teaching Lodge Ron
Doyle POB 392 Boca Raton FL 33429-0392.

Retired Seminole/Cherokee Chief Joseph
"Bloody Shirt" Bennett 2414 Bennett Rd
Plant City Fl 33565 (813) 754-6978.

Heart of the Bear Clan Chief Ron
"Standing Bear" Coats 2558 15th Ave N
St Petersburg FL 33713 (941) 327-0088.

Southeastern Cherokee Confederacy Chief
"Morning Star" Register 2119 Garden
View Rd Sebring FL 33870 (941) 385-

0705.

Rainbow Moon Clan Pan-Am Indians White
Bear Barnard 8335 Sevigny Dr North Fort
Myers Fl 33917-1705 (941) 731-7029.

Pan-Am Indians Mockingbird Clan
Director Zan "Tse Hawe" Benham 2414
Nassau St Sarasota Fl 34231 (941) 922-
7839 or 955-2724.

Southeastern Cherokee Confederacy
Assistant Principle Chief "Red Bear"
Smith 3530 Schrock St Sarasota Fl
34239-3427 (941) 365-6054.

The Conastoga/Susquehannock Tribe Chief
David Turnbull 2596 SE Durrance St
Arcadia Fl 34266 (941) 494-6930.

Pan-Am Indians Shadow Oak Band #14 Dire
tor "Dream Catcher" Richmond 106622
Shadow Oak trail Clermont Fl 34711
(904) 394-3823.

Cherokee Unity Council Sherman Cooper
Rt 6 Box 849 Okeechobee FL 34974-9604.

United Lumbee Nation Great Lakes Band
Chief Tom "Soft Shell Turtle" Netz OH
(419) 666-3257.

Star Clan of Muscogee Creeks Chariman
Ron Ethridge Sr POB 724 Cropwell AL
35054-0724.

Cherokees of NE Alabama Chris
McLaughlin 412 3rd Ave SE Leeds AL
35094.

Cherokee of Southeast Alabama Chief
Jeome Haley 2221 Rocky Ridge Rd Hoover
AL 35216 (205) 979-7019.

111

Echota Cherokee Tribe of Alabama Chief
Joe Stewart POB 190103 Birmingham AL
35216 (205) 663-2196.

The Free Cherokees Eagle Bear Band
Chief Dove Wanda Tice Rt 2 Box 310
Hamilton AL 35570 (205) 921-2589.

Wolf Clan KBTI Dwain "FiveStar" Justus
Rt 3 Box 171 Flat Rock AL 35966.

Cherokees of Jackson City POB 41 Higdon
AL 35979-0041.

Alabama Indian Affairs Commission Vice
Chairman Irne Carter POB 145 Brundidge
AL 36010-0145.

Star Clan of Muscogee Creeks Chief Erma
Lois Davenport POB 126 Goshen AL 36035-
0126 (205) 484-3589.

Alabama Indian Affairs Comission
Executive Director Darla F Graves 669 S
lawrence St Montgomery Al 36130 (800)
436-8261 FAX (205) 240-3408.

Alabama Indian Affairs Comission Sen
Danny Corbett POB 789 Phenix City AL
36130-0789.

Cherokee of Southeast Alabama Chief
Gloria Wallace POB 717 Dothan Al 36302-
0717 (205) 578-5390.

Cherokee of Southeast Alabama Violet
Hamilton 1315 Northfield Circle Dothan
Al 36303.

United Cherokee Trib of Alabama 49
Nathan Dr Daleville Al 36322.

Machis Lower Alabama Creeks Chief
Pennie Wright Rt 1-708 S John St New

Brockton AL 36351 (205) 894-5631.

Poarch Band of Creek Indians Chairman Eddie Tullis HCR 69-A Box 85-B Atmore AL 36502 (205) 368-9136 FAX (205) 368-4502.

Alabama Indian Affairs Commission Rep Jeff Dolbare Star Route Box 17 Bigbee AL 36510.

Alabama Indian Affairs Commission Bill Flucard 13130 Border Dr Grand Bay AL 36541.

Mowa Band of Choctaw Indians Chief Framon Weaver 1080 W Red Rd Mt Vernon AL 36560 (205) 829-5500 FAX (205) 829-5008.

Cumberland Creek Indian Confederation P O Box 140114 Nashville TN 37214.

Original Cherokee Nation Ruby Roberts POB 841 Hendersonville TN 37075-0841.

The Eigth Arrow Tribe Chief Paul White Feathers Russell POB 352 Lafayette TN 37083-0352.

Native Americans of Roaring River Chief Stone Bear Holly Fowler 269 Thorne Ct Lebanon TN 37087 (615) 449-8958.

White River Band Charles & Doris Ricard 1506 Cypress Dr Murfresboro TN 37130 (615) 895-6529.

Elk Valley Intertribal Cary Wade King 330 Shadow Lane Belvidere TN 37306 (615) 567-4622.

TN River Band Cherokee Outpost Gary Bass 2948 Warren Chapel Decherd TN

37324 (615) 967-5681.

Chickamauga Cherokees Chief Jim Red Eagle Reynolds 27 Honey Lane Estill Springs TN 37330 (615) 967-4191.

Veterans Band Free Cherokees Richard Maloney 561 Edith Hammond Lane Grandview TN 37337.

The Free Cherokees Chief Grey Eagle Flynn 615 Jolly Rd Grandview TN 37337 (615) 365-9965.

Cherokee Unity Council Wilma Jean Phillips POB 208 Guild TN 37340 (615) 942-6925.

Elk Valley Intertribal Chickamouga Suzil Sumech 520 A Street Hillsboro TN 37342 (615) 596-3032.

Wolf Clan KBTI Ray "Running Warrior" Gass 132 Oller Lane Hixson TN 37343.

Original Cherokee Nation Mary Green Hartman 7106 Shirley Lane Hixson TN 37343 (615) 842-2823.

Free Cherokee TN River Band Chickamauga Chief "Standing Bear" Lehr 158 Pleasant View Rd Jasper TN 37347 (615) 942-5406.

Five Nations Band Free Cherokees Jerry Manasco Baptist Hill Loop Jasper TN 37347.

Red clay Inter-Tribal Indian Band Iona Nelkirk 7703 Georgetown Rd Ooltewah TN 37363 (615) 238-9346.

TN River Band Chickamauga Cherokee Chief Golanv Ahwl Brown 9001 Bill Reed Rd #6 Ooltewah TN 37363 (615) 855-2909.

Marion County Park Ranger Ferdella Smith POB 5 Sequatchie TN 37374.

Cherokee Unity Council Heul D King Natural Bridge RD Sewannee TN 37375.

Five Nations Free Cherokees Bob A Hughes 690 Crownover Rd Sherwood TN 37369 (615) 598-0489.

Cherokee Unity Council Deanna Hayes 2021 Port Royal Dr Soddy-Daisy TN 37379.

Cherokee Unity Council Medeline C Brewer 1971 Long Island RD South Pittsburgh TN 37380 (615) 837-7202.

Inter-Tribal Rainbow Warriors Chief Lee "Bear" Trevino 201 Gentry ST Tullahoma TN 37388-3872 (615) 967-0821.

Cherokee Unity Council Shirely M Braziel 149 Horace Smith RD Whitwell TN 37397 (615) 942-5984.

Cherokee Unity Council Corliss (Gober) Lawler 704 Tremont ST Chattanooga TN 37412-9808.

Tennessee River Band of Chickamauga Mark Norman Ugaku Gigege 2624 Forest RD Chattanooga TN 37406 (615) 842-2823.

Original Cherokee Nation Senior Chief Dale F Cook POB 9808 Chattanooga TN 37412-9808.

Chickamauga Circle Free Cherokees Marty Landis POB 8113 Chattanooga TN 37414-0113.

Wolf Clan KBTI Devera Running Deer Tinker 1200 Browns Ferry Rd Chattanooga

TN 37419 (615) 821-5815.

The Chattanooga InterTribal Association
1634-A Lancer Lane Chattanooga TN
37421-3411 (Voice Mail 615/954-2376).

Tennessee River Band of Chickamauga
Cherokee Chief David Brown POB 21610
Chickamuga Station TN 37424-0610 (615)
855-8501.

Tennessee Native American Council Karen
& Bulmoose Speed POB 747 Clinton TN
37717-0747.

United Eastern Lenape Band/Middle
Division Chief Mark Little Bear RT 1
Box 22 Winfield TN 37892.

Tennessee band of Cherokee Secretary
Aufrey 405 East Red Bud Dr Knoxville TN
37920-5139 (615) 677-9559.

Wolf River Council Chief Harlen Draper
Jr POB 295 Rossville TN 38066-0295.

Cherokee Nation of Texas Loren V Hughes
7628 Hollow Fork Rd Germantown TN
38138-1740.

Cherokee Unity Council Tom "seven
Hawks" Pisut Rt 1 box 333 Granville Tn
38564.

Free Cherokees/star Hawk Band Director
Walks-Far-Wolf 1926 Catalina Dr Jackson
MS 39204 (601) 371-8242.

Red Road Indian Council Chief Gabriek
Taul Rt 1 Box 130A Hardinsburg KY
40143.

Southeastern Cherokee Confederacy Chief
Oscar "Crazy Wolf" Koskins Rt 2 Box 605

Evarts KY 40828-7902.

Southeastern Cherokee Confederacy Otter Band Chief Gaile Dark Wind Fee POB 131 Loyall KY 40854-0131 (606) 573-5927 FX (606) 573-5701.

Southeastern Cherokee Confederacy Black Wolf Band and Warrior Society POB 221 Wallins Creek KY 40873-0221 Willie & Georgia Burkhart (606) 573-9350.

United Scioto Fire Ani-Yun-Wiya Betty Jo Barnes 330 Mohave Dr Circleville OH 43113.

United Eastern Lenape Nation Big House Peoples Band POB 30648 Gahanna OH 43230-0648 Chief Alan "White Eagle" Lewis (614) 337-9494.

Bear tribe Contact person Jacqui Welker 6109 Franklin Blvd Cleveland OH 44102 (216) 651-1804.

Northeastern US Miami Council Chief Frank Sanchez 1535 Florencedale Youngstown OH 44505 (216) 746-4956.

United Eastern Lenape Band Cindy Gray Wolf Hannah 1313 Roxford St SE New Philadelphia OH 44663.

United Eastern Allegheny Nation 7797 Millersburg Rd Wooster OH 44691 War Chief Stephen "Black Crow" Marks (216) 264-1646.

Allegheny Nation Indian Center Chief William Kennedy Jr 2501 Mahoning Rd NE Canton OH 44705-1943.

Big Horn Lenape Nation Chief Black Wolf Sukatame c/o Mess 1056 West Rd

Martinsville OH 45146-9550 (513) 685-2703.

Big Horn Lenape Nation Village of Rising Wings q193 E main St #228 Chillicothe OH 45601.

Hokshicankiya Community Chief Thomas Sunhawk 25400 State Route 93 Creola OH 45622-9727 (614) 596-5371.

United Scioto Ani-Yun-Wiya Gene Anne Spirit Moon POB 23 Londonderry OH 45647-0233 (614) 884-4803.

Amonsoquath Tribe of Cherokee Deputy Chief "Shadow Walker" Jones 1540 ST Patrick Dr Elkhart IN 46514.

Miami Indian Council 641 Buchanan St Huntingdon IN 46750.

Upper Kispoko Band of Shawnee Indians Chief Augustus Rosemont 1118 Sycamore St Kokomo IN 46901-4922 (317) 457-5376.

Miami Indians of Indiana Chief Raymond White Jr POB 41 Peru IN 46970-0041 (317) 457-9631.

The Willow Pond Chief John "Grey Wolf" Self POB 458 English TN 47118-0458.

Bear Tribe Contact CAndice Jonas 21227 Midaway Southfield MI 48075 (810) 356-3625.

Swan Creek Black River Confederated Ojibway Chief Gerald Gould 1312 Oakridge #121 East Lansing MI 48823.

Grand River Ottawas Gunlakw & Colony Bands Cief William Church 21 Grand River Sr Grand Ledge MI 48837.

The Free Cherokees National Veterans Band Chief Turtle Hatching 4575 Sycamore Holt MI 48842 (517) 694-7914.

Potawatomi Tribe of Michigan & Indiana 31 Wildwood Dr Dowagiac MI 49047 (618) 424-5553.

Huron Potawatomi Band Chief David Mackety 2221 1-1/2 Mile Rd Fulton MI 49052 (616) 729-5151.

Michigan Intertribal Association Presidnt Richard Snake POB 512 Galesburg MI 49053-0512 Editor Steve Humiston 3173 Mill Creek Dr Kalamazoo MI 49009.

Pokagon Band of Potawatomi Indians Chief Daniel Rapp 53237 Town Hall Rd Dowaglac MI 49057 (616) 782-6323.

Grand River Ottawa Nation Chief Mark Kokx 200 Peach Ave Hart MI 49420.

Ottawa tribe of Northern Michigan 1391 Terrace St Muskegon MI 49441 (517) 354-3442.

Burt Lake Band of Ottawa & Chippewa Indians Chief Donald A Morre 4371 Indian Rd Brutus MI 49716 (616) 529-6564.

Little Traverse Bay Bands of Odawa Indians Chief Ronald Wemigwasw PB 130 Cross Village MI 49723-0130 Frank Ettawageshik (616) 263-7141.

Lake Superior Chippewa of Marquette Chief Donald Bressette POB 1071 Marquette MI 49855-1071.

Chippewa Indian Tribe Lac Vieux Desert

Band of Lake Superior POB 249
Watersmeet MI 49969-0446 (906) 358-4577
FAX (906) 358-4785.

Bear Tribe Contact Debra Perez
Grosswald 311 W broadway Fairfield IA
52556 (515) 472-7377.

Bear Tribe Contact Joya Banaka & Joann
Chambers POB 1946 Fairfield IA 52556-
1946 (515) 472-4587.

Brotherton Indians of Wisconsin Chief
June Ezold 2848 Witches Lake Rd
Woodruff WI 54568 (715) 542-3913.

Bear Tribe Contact Holly Gray-Schuck
3408 16th Ave S Minneapolis MN 55407
(612) 722-2637.

Little Shell Tribe of North Dakota
Chief Ron Delorme POB 173 Rolette ND
58366-0173.

Little Shell Tribe of Montana Chippewa
Indians Chief Debbie Swanson 426 W
Quartz Butte MT 59701 (406) 265-2741.

Bear Tribe Contact Person Elena Shahan
5027 Eastside Hwy Stevensville MT 59870
(406) 777-3402.

Pan Am Indians The Shadow Nation Chief
Shadow Walker POB 106 New Baden IL
62256-0106 (618) 588-4590.

Amonsoquath Tribe of Cherokees Medicine
Man Jim Groves 2422 Hope St Hannibal MO
63401-3833.

Hanapapa Pipe Clan Amonsoquath Tribe
Judge Harold Urton RT 2 Box 230
Lewiston MO 63452.

Amonsoquath Tribe/ Hanapapa Pipe Clan
Chief Charles White RR 2 Box 188
Palmyra MO 63452.

Amonsoquath Tribe of Cherokee Prin
Chief Walking Bear Wilson HCR 1 Box 127
Van Buren MO 63965-9801.

The Northern Cherokee Nation c/o Chief
Griggs 578 E Highway #7 Clinton MO
64735-9511.

United Lumbee Nation Black Bear Clan
Chief Jeannie Franks 2510 Markwardt St
Joplin MO 63801-5352.

The Free Cherokees Dogwood Band Chief
Dancing Crane Rt 1-1151 Nashville
Church Rd Ashland MO 65010 (314) 657-
9004.

Red Tail Alliance Sunny Mundy POB 1872
Jefferson City MO 65102-1872 Publishes
Earth Bridge.

The Free Cherokees Hummingbird Clan
Chief Sitting Wolf 1109 E Walnut St
Columbia MO 65102.

N Cherokees of Old Louisianna Territory
Chief Beverly Northrup 1502 E Broadway
#201 Columbia MO 65102 (314) 443-2424.

The Free Cherokees Hummingbird Clan
Chief Nation Pathfinder 1109 E Walnut
St Columbia MO 65102.

Chickamauga Cherokee Nation Will T
Gunier POB 95 Rocheport MO 65279-0095
(314) 698-2097.

United Lumbee Nation Black Bear Clan
Talking Bear 18146 Universal Dr Falcon
MO 65470.

Pan AM Indians Mo 22 Spirit of the Four Winds Tribe 313 W Commercial St #B Lebanon MO 65536-3105 Medicine Chief Jerry Fincher (417) 588-1412.

Chickamauga Cherokee Nation MO/AP White River Band Bobbie L Sanders 106 S Calhoun Ave Ash MO 65604 (417) 751-3422.

Chickamauga Cherokee Nation MO/AP White River Band Leonard & Junie Epps POB 932 Ava MO 65609-0931 (417) 683-2421.

Chickamauga Cherokee Nation Chief Donald E Coones Chairman Rt 2 Box 2029 Fair Play MO 65649 (417) 654-4003.

Chickamauga Cherokee Nation Richard Craker 501 Front Rd 2030 Monett MO 65708 (417) 235-5082.

Powhatan Clan Amonsoquath Tribe Judge John Wilson 956 Towbridge Rd Sparta MO 65753.

Amonsoquath Tribe of Cherokee Powhatan Clan Chief Shining Bear Furr POB 962 Towbridge Sparta MO 65753-0962 (417) 634-3644.

Southwest Missouri Indian Center Exec Director Mike Fields 2422 West Division Springfield MO 65802.

Delaware-Munci Tribe Chief Clio Church POB 274 Pomono KS 66076-0274.

Kaweah Indian Nation of W USA & Mexico Chief Thunderbird IV Webber POB 3121 Hutchinson KS 67504-3121 (316) 665-3614 Native American Church.

United Houma Nation Chief Laura Billiot

POB 127 Dulal LA 70353-0127 (514) 851-1550.

Deer Clan of Louisianna Chief Yellow Fawn Rt 4 Box 87-2 Farmersville LA 71241 (318) 368-2717.

Jena Band of Chocktaw Chariman Jerry D Jackson PB 14 Jena LA 71445 (318) 992-2717.

Clifton Chocktaws Indians Chief Henry Neal 1068 Clifton Rd More LA 71445 (318) 793-8796.

Caddo Adais Indians Chief Rufus Davis Jr Rt 2 Box 246 Robeline LA 71469 (318) 472-8680.

Chocktaw-Apache Tribe of Ebarb Community 9f Ebarb Tribal Chairman Tommy Bolton POB 858 Zwoile LA 71486 (318) 645-2744.

The Free Cherokees Dung Beetle society Willie Touches Earth Rutledge Rt 1 Box 256 Portland AR 71663 (501) 737-2381.

Deer Clan of LA Deer Tracks Robinson 124 Robinson Lane #B El Dorado AR 71730-8972.

The Revived Ouachita Indians Council Elder Debert Hammer Graves 1001 Emory St Hot Springs AR 71901.

Ouachita Indians of Arkansas Genad Head Chief Loren Great Eagle Long POB 1026 Hot SPrings AR 71902-1026 (510) 624-6796 FAX at Image World (501) 624-5262.

The Revived Ouachita Indians Council Elder William Wren Wren 2156 Higdon

Ferry RD Hot Springs AR 71913.

The Revived Ouachita Indians Council
Elder Dale Wounded Bear Ivy POB 137
Donaldson AR 71941-0137.

The Revived Ouachita Indians Chris Sea
Bear Norris Northside Apr #20 Glenwood
AR 71943.

The Revived Ouachita Indians Andrew
Healer Rublly POB 938 Mount Ida AR
71957-0938.

Trails of Tears Association Jim
Walsmith 1100 N University Ste 113
Little Rock AR 72207-6344.

The Free Cherokees Chief Whitefeather
POB 641 Helena AR 72342-0641 (510) 338-
7966.

The Free Cherokees Ark Bear Tribe Band
Chief Medicine Bearman HC 72 Box 210
Mountain home AR 72560-9505 (501) 481-
5394.

Revived Ouachitas Clarence Running
Water Sargent 7548 Batesville Blvd c/o
Tufor Pleasant Plains AR 72568.

Chickamaauga Cherokee Nation Princess
Sharon Thompson Rt 2 Box 647 Green
Forest AR 72638 (510) 423-6464.

The Free Cherokees Good Medicine Band
Director Grandmother Alloday Taylor POB
449 Norfolk AR 42658-0449 (501) 499-
8083/Publishes the Flowering Tree
Newsletter 4 issues $8.

Chickamauga Cherokee Nation White River
Band James & Irene Johnson HCR 67 Box
41 - B Waldron AR 72958 (501) 637-2383.

Northern Cherokee Tribe Chief Beverly A Baker 412 7th St Weatherford AR 73096-4712.

Chickamauga Cherokee Nation MO/AR Hazel Hall 1509 SW 35th St Oklahoma City OK 73119-2241 (405) 232-3033.

Chickamauga Cherokee Nation MO/AR White River Band Oscar Johnson 10001 Tralfalgar Oklahoma City ON 73139 (405) 691-1654.

Delaware Tribe of Eastern Oklahoma Chief Lewis Ketchum 108 South Seneca Bartlesville OK 74005 (918) 336-5272.

Chickamauga Cherokee Nation MO/AR White River Band Burtie & Thelma Dale 323 N 5th St Jenks OK 74037 (918) 299-5207.

Yuchi Tribe Chief Al Roland POB 1990 Sapulpa OK 74067-1990.

Cherokee Unity Council Nancy Madriel White Feather Dove Rt 2 Box 185 Tahlequah OK 74464.

Keetoowah Cherokee Indians Chief John Ross POB 746 Tahlequah OK 74465-0746 (918) 456-9462 FAX (918) 456-3648.

Chickamauga Cherokee Nation MO/AR White River Band Larry Johnson 615 Ponderson Dr Chandler OK 74834 (405) 258-2073.

Chickamauga Cherokee Nation MO/AR White River Band Jim & anita Slayton 34516 E W 96th Chandler OK 74834 (918) 866-2533.

Chickamauga Cherokee Nation MO/AR White River Band Max & clara Robbins Rt 1 Box 115-B Sparks OK 74869 (918) 866-2213.

Free Cherokee Hummingbird Clan Chief
Nathan Couch Pathfinder 2214 Wren Lane
Lewisville Tx 75067 (214) 317-1992.

Cherokee Nation of Texas Principle
Chief Utsidihi Hicks 505 East McKay
Troup Tx 75789 (903) 842-3329.

Texas Cherokee Tsalagiyi Nvdagi POB 492
Troup TX 75789-0492.

The Eagle Clan Chief Teddy Grey Hawk
Davis Jr 508 Elizabeth Lane Mansfield
TX 76063 (817) 473-4013.

Alabama Coushatta Tribes Rt 3 Box 640
Livingston Tx 77351 (409) 563-4391 FAX
563-4397.

The Cherokee Cultural Society of
Houston Pres Deborah Scott POB 1506
Bellaire TX 77402.

Cherokee Unity Council Dr Everett &
Marlene Treadway 2911 Texas Ave South
College Station TX 77845 (409) 693-
0656.

Tigua Yslleta Del Sur Tiwa Tribe POB
17579 Ysleta Station El Paso TX 79917-
7579 (915) 859-7913 FAX 859-2988.

Bear Tribe Contact Person Tom Stevens
9108 Mandel St Denver Co. 80221 Ph/Fax
(303) 427-7088 Email
tomtrainer@aol.com.

Pan-Am Indians Little Bear Tribe Chief
Jack Rabbit Schnetzler 2056 Odin Dr
Silt CO 81652 (303) 876-5896.

The Revived Ouachita Indians Council
Elder Clara Three Paths Williams 226
Adams St Chubbuck ID 83202-2108.

Bear Tribe Contact Person Guy Neidermier 1726 Luker Rd Kuna ID 83634.

NE Shoshone Indians 660 South 200 West Brigham City UT 84302.

Cherokee Family Ties President Donna Williams 516 N 38th St Mesa AZ 85205.

Deer tribe Metis Medicina Society CEO Janneke Koole 11259 E Via Linda #100-142 Scottsdale AZ 85259-4706.

United Lumbee Nation Eagle Clan Helen Little Princess Beck POB 306 Quartzsite AZ 85346-0306 (602) 927-4288.

Munsee Thames River Delaware Tribe Chief Little Soldier HC1 Box 1909 Tucson AZ 85736.

Pascua Yaqui San Ignacio YaquiCouncil Inc 7474 S Camino De Oeste Tucson AZ 85746 (602) 883-2838.

United Lenape Nation Chief Robert Three Eagles Shrewsbury POB 1198 Fredonia AZ 86022-1198 (307) 332-2660.

Bear Tribe Contact Person Zhenya Jane Rice Pob 298 Sedona AZ 86336-0298 (602) 284-9481.

Canoncito Band of Navajos Chief Leon Secatero POB 498 Canoncito NM 87026-0498 (505) 836-7141.

San Juan de Guadalupe Tiwa Tribe 559 West Brown Rd Las Cruses NM 88001.

Pahrump Band of Paiutes Chief Richard Arnold POB 73 Pahrump NV 89041-0073 (702) 647-5842/727-6559.

Coastanoan Band of Carmel Mission
Indians Chief Anthony Miranda POB 1657
Monrovia CA 91016-1657.

Bear Tribe Contact Person Glen
Schliffman 2308 Clark Ave Burbank CA
91506 (818) 846-3043 Email
qbfgjs@earthlink.net.

Jamul Band POB 612 Jamul CA 91935-0612
(619) 669-4785 FAX 669-4817.

Atahun Shoshones of San Juan Capistrano
2352 Bahia Dr La Jolla Ca 92037.

Shadowlight Medicine Clan Dr Medicine
Hawk Wilburn 2065 W College Ave #2105
San Bernadidno CA 92407-4655 (909) 883-
1212.

Juaneno Band of Mission Indians Chief
David Belardes 31742 Via Belardes San
Juan Capistrano CA 92675 (714) 493-
4933.

Coastal band of Chumash Indians Chief
Frances Franco 610 Del Monte Ave Santa
Barbara CA 93101 (805) 965-0718.

Kern Valley Indian Community Chief
Ronald Wermuth POB 168 Kernville CA
93238-0168 (619) 376-3761.

United Lumbee Nation Bear Clan Chief
Ben Screaming Bear Bailey 3427 West
Monte Vista Visaila CA 93277.

United Lumbee Nation P O Box 1629
Fontana Ca 92334-1629.

Ani-Yun-Wiya Society POB 1921
Bakersfield CA 93301-1921.

Mono Lake Indian Community Chief Jerry

Andrews POB 237 Lee Vining CA 935410237
(619) 647-6471.

Cherokee Renegade Society Chief Marion
Morgan C/o Jim Brothers 38636 Division
St Palmdale CA 93550 (805) 267-2921.

Tehatchapi Indian Tribe 219 E H St
Tehatchapi Ca 93561.

Dunlap Band of Mono Indians Chief
Florence Dick POB 344 Dunlap CA 93621-
0344 (209) 338-2842.

Amah Band of Ohlone/Costanoan Indians
Chief Irene Zwierlein 789 Canada Rd
Woodside CA 94062 (415) 851-7757FAX
851-7489.

North Fork Band of Mono Indians Chief
Ron Goode POB 120 San Francisco CA
84121-0120 (415) 752-9085.

Esselen Tribe of Monterey Chief Jopan
Denys 3012 Rosalie St San Mateo Ca
94403 (415) 570-6496.

Indian Canyon Band of Coastanoan/mutsun
Indians Chief Ann Marie Sayers POB 28
Hollister CA 95024-0028.

Muwekma Ohlone tribe Chief Rosemary
Cambra 1845 The Alameda San Jose CA
95113 (408) 293-9956.

Salinan Nation Chief Jennie McLeod POB
610-546 San Jose CA 95161-0546 (408)
923-1315.

Miwok Indian Band Star Rt 1 West Point
Ca 95255.

Mariposa Indian Council Chief Nicholas
Broochini POB 1200 Mariposa CA 95318-

1200 (209) 966-3126.

The Chickchansi Yokotch Tribe Chief
Lydia L Appling 4962 Wat Rd Mariposa CA
95338-9743 (209) 742-7060.

United Lumbee Nation War Hawk Band
Chief Sly Fox Quigle 2308 McRitchie Way
Modesto CA 95355.

The Revived Ouachita Indians Messenger
Scout Dorothy Bee Scout Cox 470 Derby
Lane Santa Rosa CA 95404.

Yokayo Pomo Rancheria Chief Dorene
Mitchell 1114 Helen Ave Unkiah Ca 95482
(707) 462-4074.

Pan Am Indians #19 Thunderbird Clan
Chief Ojala 111 Orchard Lane Charlotta
CA 95528 Office (707) 768-3226.

Tolowa-tututni Indians Audrey Bowen POB
213 Fort Dick CA 95538-0388 (707) 464-
7332.

Tsnungwe Council Chief Charles Ammon
POB 373 Salyer CA 95563-0373 (916) 629-
3356.

Hownonquet Community Association POB
239 Smith River CA 95567-0239.

The Free Cherokees Contact Star Dancer
BOX 1599 Sutter Creek Ca 95685-1599
(209) Home 267-0507 Work 0519 FAX 5144.

Northern Maidu Tribe POB 217 Greenville
CA 95947-0217.

Wintoon Indians Chief Isabell F Grant
4030 Churn Creek RD Redding CA 96002-
3631.

Big Meadows Lodge Tribe POB 362 Chester CA 96020-0362.

United Lumbee Nation Chieftainess Silver Star Reed POB 512 Fall River Mills CA 96028 (916) 336-6701.

Hayfork Band of Nor-El-Muk Wintu Indians Chief Raymond Patton POB 968 Hayfork CA 96041-0968 (916) 628-5175.

Wintu Tribe of N California Chair Wayne Lievsay POB 71036 Project City CA 96079-1036 Carol Martin (916) 243-1766.

Shasta Tribe Chief Roy V Hail POB 1054 Yreka CA 96097-1054 (916) 842-5654.

Washoe/Paiute of Antelope Valley Chief Wesley Dick POB 52 Colleville CA 96107-0052 (916) 495-2824.

Antelope Valley Paiute Tribe Chief Bill Lovett Box 119 Colleville CA 96107-0119 (916) 266-3126.

Maidu Nation Chief Clara LeCompte POB 204 Susanville CA 96180-0204 (916) 257-9691.

Native American Center Director Melody Charlie POB 226 Hauula HI 96717-0226 (808) 293-9042.

Bear Tribe Contact Person Dr Judith Boice 11520 SE main St Portland OR97216 (503) 252-6492.

Chetco Tribe 564 Fern St Brokkins OR 97415 (503) 469-7131.

Confederated Tribes of Coos Lower Umpquah and Siuslaw Indians 445 S 4th St Coos Bay OR 97420 (503) 267-5454 FAX

269-1647.

Coquille Indian Tribe POB 1435 Coos Bay OR 97420-1435 (503) 888-4274 FAX 269-2573.

NW Cherokee Confederacy Wolf Band Chief Robert Cilver Badger Ponder 3003 State St #23 Medford OR 97504 (503) 535-5406.

Tchinouk Indians Chief Karleen Parazoo 5621 Al;tamont Sr Klamath Falls OR 97601 (503) 884-3844.

Klamath Tribe POB 436 Chiloquin OR 97624-0436 (503) 783-2219 FAX 783-2029.

Duwamish Tribe Chief Cecille Maxwell 212 Wells Ave S #C Renton WA 98055-2142.

Northwest Five Tribes Association Director Linda She My Hope Knighton POB 85072 Seattle Wa 98145-5072.

Pan Am Indians Butterfly Clan Lord Richerd Badger Chief Totem 329 S 177th St #E304 Seattle WA 98148-2703.

Samish Tribe Chief Margaret Greene POB 217 Anacourtes W 98221-0217 (206) 293-6404.

Bear Tribe Contact Person Dawn Feathersong Davies 18015 Dubuque Rd Snohomish WA 98290 (360) 568-1358.

Steilacoom Tribe Chief Joan Ortez POB 419 Steilacoom WA 98388-0419 (206) 847-6448.

The Free Cherokees 4 Directions Council Chief Harvest Moon 175 Smokey Valley Rd RToledo WA 98591 (206) 864-4601.

Snoqualmoo Tribe of Whidbey Island
Chief Lon Posenjak 1321 Baker Ave N
East Wenachee WA 98802-4334.

Bear Tribe Contact Person Mary Ann
Little Bear {POB 1022 Tum Tum Wa 99034-
1022.

Bear Tribe Contact Person Trishawa *
Stephen Buhner POB 1147 Tum Tum WA
99034-1147 (509) 258-9148.

Bear Tribe Contact Person Crysallis
Mulligan West 1727 Northwest Blvd #33
Spokane WA 99205 (509) 325-4113.

The Bear Tribe Main Office POB 9167
Spokane WA 99209-9167 (509) 326-4505.

Bear Tribe Contact Person Sonya
Riversong POB 2464 Walla Walla WA
99362-2464.

Southeastern Cherokee Confederacy
Councilman John Brave Bear Crowder POB
520348 Big Lake AK 99652-0348 (907)
892-8203.

Southeastern Cherokee Confederacy Lilly
Tawahna Berg POB 54 Soldotna AK 99669-
0054.

Oneida Tribe of Indians of Wisconsin P
O Box 365 Oneida WI 54155.

Oneida Community Library C/O Oral
Tradition P O Box 365 Elm St Oneida WI
54155.

Terrence Nelson Box 346 Letelier
Manitoba Canada ROG 1CO (204) 427-2312.

Roseau River Anishinabe First Nation P
O Box 30 Ginew Manitoba Canada ROA 2RO.

Ho Chunk Nation of Wisconsin P O Box 667 Black River Falls WI 54615.

Gila River Community Box 38 Sacaton Az 85247.

Oneida Nation of New York 1-800-685-6115.

Oneida Nation of Wisconsin 1-800-236-2214.

Bar River Ojibwa P O Box 51 Odanah WI 54861 (715) 682-7893 (715) 682-7894.

INDEX I

NATIVE AMERICAN ANCESTORS

ADAMS - Ann Jane 2,3, Anna Jane 2, 3,
Anne Jane 2, 3, Annie Jane 2, Lydia
(Licenbegler Ostandes Pierce) 2, 3, 4,
52, 61, 63, Samuel D. 2, 3, 4, 52, 61,
63, Sarah 4.

ALFORD - 5.

ALLEN - Betsy 5, Elihu 5, Rachel 5,
Zebulon 6.

ALLISON (Ellison) - Elizabeth(?) 6.

ALLSHOUSE - Elizabeth 6, Finley 2, 3,
4, 6, Henry Jr. 6, Henry Sr. 6, John
Jr. 7, John Sr. 7, Leona Lowden 7, Mary
7, Susannah(?) 7.

ALMOND - William 7.

ANDRE - Statton Tecumseh 8.

ASH - (Moye) Clara Belle 8, Doris Mae
8.

BAKER - Alvin 9, Amanda 9, Angela 8,
Arthur 9, Arthur Sydney 9, Barbara 9,
Barry 9, Ben 9, Benjamin 10, Benny 10,
Bruce 10, Charles 10, Charles H 10,
Charley 11, Clarence Robert 11,
Clarissa 10, Dale Alan 10, Dana 11,
David 11, David Hiram 11, Debby Tabor
11, Delcy 11, Diane 11, Dinemis
(Dennis?) 12, Eleanor 12, Electa 12,
Eliza Ann 12, Ellen 12, Emma 12, Ethel
12, Fanny Elizabeth 12, Gary Richard
13, Gideon 13, Gregory 13, Hannah 13,
Hiram 13, Hulda 13, Isabelle Louise
Darrah 13, Jeffrey 14, John 14,
Katherine 14, Kaye 14, Kenneth Levander
14, Lancyma (Luna) 14, Lavina (Luenna?)
14, Levander 14, Louise 15, Lydia 15,
Marion Isabel 14, Mary 15, Matilda 16,
Mercy(?) 16, Michael 16, Nicholas 16,

Orison 16, Otto 16, Robert 16, Rodney
Brett 17, Ronald 17, Rueben 17, Ruth
Ann 17, Sally (Betsy) Elizabeth 17,
Samantha Hathaway 17, Sara 18, Sharon
Lynn 18, Susan 18, Susie J. 18, Stephen
18, Thomas 18, Thomas Jr. 18, Thomas
18, Thomas III 19, Thomas Jr. 19, Vada
19, Virgina T 19, Walter Richard 19.

BALL - Rebbecca Hoagland 19.

BANKS - Anne 20.

BARNES - Lula 20.

BASS - Rice 20.

BOURASSA - Daniel 20.

BOWEN - Lucinda 21, Perin Tyre 21.

BROWN - Frances 21, Mary Jane 21.

BUCK - Mariah 22.

BURNETT - Abram 22.

CABLER - Mary E 22.

CAMPBELL - Alexander 22, Andrew Hawkins
23, David 24, Isabella 24, John 24,
Nancy 25, William 25.

CAUDILL - Elizabeth 26, Stephen 26.

CHANCY - Rachel 26.

CHRISTIE - Carolyn Isabel 26, John
Edwin 26, Louise 26, Margaret 27, Maria
27, Marion Isabel 27, William Wallace
27.

CLARK - Iris Lorraine Stewart 28.

COLLIER - Dianah 28.

COLLINS - George W. Jr 28, George W. Sr 28, Robert 29, Thomas 29.

COOPER - Mollie 30.

COX - Emma 30.

CRUIT - Anne Garrison 31.

CUNNINGHAM - Carolyn Isabel 31, Deborah Louise 31, James 31, Richard David 31, Steven 32.

DANIELS - Sally (Betsy) Elizabeth 32.

DAY - Loutisha 32.

DEMPSEY - Simion Arledge 33.

DICK - Donald 33, Jane Pauline 33.

DOWDEN - Nancy/Ann ? 34.

DUNCAN, Ida Pinina 35.

DUNN - Thomas Spencer 35.

ELLISON (Allison) - Susanna 35.

EDWARDS - Elder Norman 36, Esther Matilda 36, John 36, John Henry 37.

ESTECHACKO - Menawz 37.

FOX - Amy Ann 37, James 37.

FRANKLIN - Elizabeth 38.

GARNER - Mary A (m. to William Robbins) 39.

GREEN - James Robert "Hunting Horse" 39, Gordon/Gardener 39, /Harbeston 39.

HAWK - Keziah 409.

HENDRIX - Carol 42, Thomas 43.

HOWARD - John or Thomas 43.

HURST - Clifford 43.

ISDELL - Willie Estelle 44.

JERNIGAN - Mary 45.

JOHNSON - Anna Catherine 45, Barbara 46, Cinthia Ann 47, Silas 47.

JONES - Alann 47, Christopher 48, Marisa Louise 48, Melanie Ann 49, Phebe Ann 49, Richard 49, Robert Aaron 50, Scott 50.

KING - Adam Meek 51, Mary Sue 451

KINNEY - Lillian 51

LEE - Catherine 52.

LICENBEGLER - Lydia 2, 3, 4, 52, 61, 63.

LOSEY - 52.

LOUDERBACH - Anne G. 53.

MALONE - Andrew J 53, Thomas Monroe 53.

MARSH - Charles 54, Dave A. 54, Dora Catherine 55.

MATHENY - William 55.

MCABE - Mary 55.

MCAFOOSE - Catherine (River/Shriver)
57.

MEEK - Margaret 57.

METEA - 57.

MITCHELL - Florence 58, Francis Jane
58, Harry Lee 58, Harry R 58, Leona
59.

MOYE - Joe (Joseph) Jefferson 59.

NAVARRE - Pierre 59.

NEEDLES - John 60.

NICKOLS - William Edward 60.

NIXON - Willaim 60.

O'QUINN - Tyler 61.

OSTANDER - Lydia Adams 2, 3, 4, 52, 61,
63.

OSTANDES - Lydia Adams 2, 3, 4, 52, 61,
631.

OURY - Catherine (Frantz) 61.

OVERTON - David 62.

OWENS - Olivia 62.

PADGETT - Sarah 67.

PETERSON - Elizabeth (Betsy) 63.

PIERCE - Lydia Adams 2, 3, 4, 52, 61,
63.

PRITCHETT - Croman W 64.

RAGER - Michael 64.

RAYEN - John 64.

RAYMOND - Amy Grace 65.

REDING - Nancy Baker 65, Robert 65.

ROBBINS - William 66.

ROBERTS - Benny 66, Lavina (Luenna) 66,
Noah 67, Robert 67, Teackle 67.

ROGERS - Ed 68, Lancyma (Luna) 68,
Samuel Alfred 68, Sara 68, William
Haywood 69.

ROPER - Judy 69.

SHARP - Susie Leona 69.

SINCLAIR - Hugh Crige 70.

SKAIN, Nancy (?) 70.

SKIPPER - Mary Cleveland 70.

SMITH - David - Young Eagle 71, Sara
72, Sarah Nixon 74.

STALCUP - Elmer Ellsworth 74, Florence
Cordelia 74, Lottie Leona Gamble 74.

STANLEY - Caroline 75.

SULLIVAN - Ellen 75.

TERRELL - Jack 75, William Mack 76.

THORNTON - Henry 76.

TOOLE - ? Miss 76.

TUCKER - George 76.

TUTEN - Maryann Tabitha Stanley 77.

VIEUX - Louis 77.

WABAUNSEE - 78.

WALTERS - Mollie Ann 78.

WAMEGO - 78

WHITE - Benjamin 78, Eleanore Joy 79,
Elizabeth 79, Eva (Retta?) 79, Fisher
80, Garnet 80, George 81, Hannah 81
Harriet 81, Harry 82, James 82, John
82, Joseph 83, Lawn Ellis 83, Mary 83,
Matilda 84, Otto 84, Rebecca Ann 85,
Samuel 85, Sarah 85, Wesley 86, William
86, William H 87.

WILCOX - Ann 87, Carol 87, Gayle 88,
Stephen 88, Sue 88.

WILDER - Willis 88.

WILKENSON, Harriet Moss 89.

WILLIAMS - Nancy 89.

WILLIS - Kathryn 90.

WILSON - Benjamin Franklin 90.

WOODRUFF - Joshua 91.

WRIGHT - Clarisa 91, Eunice 91.

YAHULA - Elizabeth 92.

ZERRY - Thomas 92.

INDEX II

ALLIED NAMES

ADAMS - Annie 2, 42, Elizabeth 5.

ALMOND - Tum 7, John 7, Rena 7, Nancy 7, Sally 7, Elizabeth 7, Rhoda 7, Martha 7.

AMES - Mary Ann 56.

ASH - Amy Grace (Raymond) 65, Doris Mae 8, 65, Echo 65, James Linden 65, Jesse 65, Lena 65, Margaret 65, Orion Clinton 8, Pearl Urshell (Wilder) 8, Roy 65.

BAKER - Ann Nancy 65, Sara (?) 16.

BASS - Aaron 45, Barney Cone 45, Betsy 63, Charles 45, 63, Charles Bishop Jr 63, Crawford 63, Elvira 63, Eliza James 45, Etta Mary 45, Everett 63, Joseph 45, Lonnie 63, Lottie 63, Lucy Ann 45, Mary Bell 63, Moses Everett 45, Needham 20, 45, 63, Quinna 63, Robinson 63, Robert 45, 63, Selvania 63, Verna 63, Willa E. 63.

BECK - Iva Snyder 40.

BLACK - Margaret 64, Uriah 64.

BLELANSKI - Jennie 39.

BROWN - Charlie 25, John V 6, 34, Mary Jane 28, William 32.

CAMPBELL - Ace (Asa) 24, Charity Yahula 24, Elijah 24, Elizabeth 24, Ges 24, John 24, Joseph 24, Kst 24, Lacy 24, Landon 24, Mary I (Stout) 24, Minnielie 24, Onl 24, Major William 24.

COLEMAN - Eligha 24, Hannah 24, Hosea 24, Martha Jane 24, Mary Ann 24, Philip Newton 24, Sara 24, Susan 24, Valentine

24, William Marion 24.

COLLINS - Ann (Banks) 29, George W 21,
Lucinda (Tyre) 21, Mary Jane (Brown)
28, Nancy (Williams) 29, Robert 29.

COOPER - George 68, Mollie (Moye) 59.

CROWE - Margaret Anne 53.

DAMERON - Nancy 54.

DAVIS - Priscilla 97.

DEMONT - Catherine 47.

DEMPSEY - Cynthia Rosella (Tuten) 32,
Iva Annie 33, Monroe 33, Norman 33.

DOWDEN - William 34.

DUCKETT - Sula (Heaton) 44, Sidney 44.

DUNN - Alva 35, Bessie 35, Louis 35,
Margaret Virginia (McCrory) 35.

DURHAM - (Dunham), Lettie 43.

EDWARDS - Aisley (Paulson) 36, Colie
Cincinnati 37, Dora Catherine (Ash) 36,
Easer W 36, Elder Norman 37, 53, Esther
36, Esther Ann (Williams) 37, Ester
Matilda 42, Frances Etta 37, Henry 36
Ida S 37, James Thomas 36, John Henry
36, John W 37, Lena E, 37 Mildred 36,
Ollie 36, Phoebe Blanche 37, Sudie P
37, Woodrow 36.

EGGE - David 44, Shawn 44, Tiffany 44.

Estachacko - Bijwarrir 37, Charity 37,
Elizabeth 37, Garra Wynn 37, Menawa 37,
Tustanuaae Thlocko 37.

145

EVANS - Matilda A 54.

EXELL - Ellen Manerva (King) 51.

FELDER - Alice 35, Bill 35, Carl 35, Earl 35, Florence 35, Gladys 35, Ida Pinina (Duncan) 35, William Warren 35.

GAMBLE - Lottie Leona 74.

GIBSON - Sarah Ann Elizea 89, T J 89.

GIDDEONS - Beula Wilson 90.

GIDINGS - Louise (Lou) C (Wilson) 90.

GREEN - Cynthia (Cindy) 39, Iseae 39, James 39, Jennie (Blelanski) 39, John 39, Letha 39, Shelly 39, Sukie 39, Sukky ? 37, William 39. ? 39.

HAMBLETT - Moxais (Muses) 69.

HEATON - Sula (Duckett) 44.

HENRY - Patrick 53, Rebecca 53.

HILES - Brodus Owen 69, Eli Millen 53, Morgan 75.

HILLSMAN - Pearl (Isdell) 44.

HURST - Betty Ann 36, Bobby 36, Clifford 36, Julia Rae 36.

ISBILL - Isabell 45, Lillie M 45, Mary I 45, Sarah A 45.

ISDELL - Aurasphere Trinity McDonald 44, Amos Moses 44, Carmen Regina Doucette 44, Ezekiel Daniel 44, Gerri Lynn 44, Jacqueline 44, Jammey 44, James 44, Janice 44, Jeremiah Joseph

44, Joseph Sherman 44, Lacey 44,
Pauline Michelle Thomas 44, Pearl
(Hillsman) 44, Richard Marlin 44,
Samuel Eli 44, Terrell John Thomas 44.

JOHNSON - Alma 47, Anna Catherine 47,
Camelia 47, Catherine (Demont) 47,
Charles 47, George 47, Matilda 47,
William 47.

KING - Adam 57, Amy Torre 57, Danial
57, Daniel 51, Edger 51, Ellne Manawa
Exell 51, George 57, Hellen 57,
Margaret 57, Margaret (Meek) 57, Marian
51, Mary 57, Mary Sue 57, Nancy 57,
Thomas 57, Sarah 57.

LAMBERT - Leo B. 53

LANGSTON - Carrie Wilson 90.

LEE - Izek 42.

LEMONS - Donna Senora 23, Ellen B. 23,
Paralee 23, James B. 23, James K Polk
23, Julia C. 23, Mary 23, Mary E Cabler
23, Mihon T. 23, Nancy Eliza 23,
Nicholas 23, Sarah A Jane 23, & William
A. 23.

LOSEY - Holman 53 Margaret Anne (Crowe)
53, Ruby 53.

MALLONE - Charles Sincanate 51, Charles
51, Clarance 51, Oceola 51, Theodocia
51, Thomas 51.

MALONE - Andrew J 65, Berta 47, 53,
Charley 47, 53, Cinthia Ann (Johnson)
53, Eugean 47, 53 Henderson 53, 65,
Howard 47, 53, Thomas 53, 65, Thomas
Monroe 47, William 53, 65, Nancy Baker
(Reding) 53.

MARSH - Charles D 54, Capt Benjamin 54,
Dora Catherine (Edwards) 36, Wesley 54,
Edward 55, Elizabeth 54 James R 54,
Maggie 54, Matilda A (Evans) 54, Nancy
Dameron 54, Walter H 54.

MARTIN - Adela 62.

MATHENY (or Mathena) - Nathaniel 55,
Elizabeth Parker 55.

McCRONE - Missouri "Zury" Wilson
(Merritt) 90.

McCRORY - Margaret Virginia (DUNN) 35.

McDONALD - Aurasphere Trinity 45.

MECKLEY - John J 42.

MERRITT - Ella Wilson (Tillus) 90, Gena
(Wilson) 90, Missouri "Zury" Wilson
(McCrone) 90.

MIDDLETON - Chad Trevor 40, John D Jr
40.

MILLER - Kate Landusky Nickols 60.

MOYE - Clara 30, 59, Hattie 30, 59, Joe
30, 59, Joe (Joseph) Jefferson 59, John
30, 59, Mary 30, 59.

NEEDLES - Francis 60.

NICKOLS - James 60, Kate Landusky
Miller 60.

NIXON - Bertha P 61, Calvin 61, Etta 61
Gabriella (Parr) 61, Henry L. 61, Lang
N 61, Mittie E 61, Sallie Rebecca 61,
Sarah (Sally)(Smith) 60, Sarah (Sally)
74, William 74.

OVERTON - David 62, Elizabeth 62,
George 62, Henry 62, Jackson 62, Jesse
62, Mariah 62, Mary 62, Mary (Tucker)
62, Rachel 62, William 62.

OLINGER - Mary Ann 41.

O'QUINN - Barry 61, Elizabeth (Stone)
61.

PARR - Gabriella 60.

PAULSON - Aisley 36.

PHILLIPS - William 42.

PLATTS - Johnathan Edward 62.

PRITCHETT - Croman W. 70, Lucy 64, 71,
Marvin 64, 71, Mary Cleveland (Skipper)
64, Mary Lee 64, 71, S.J. 64, 71,
Verbon 64, 71.

RAGER - Susanna Wagaman 64, John 64,
Mary Jane 64, Margaret (Black) 64,
William 64.

RAYMOND - Amy 45, Jesse 45, John W. 45.

REAMER - Everett 8, Jack 8, Jane 8,
Shirley 8.

REDING - John 26, Robert 26, (Malone),
Nancy Baker 52.

ROBBINS - Amanda 39, 66, Charles 39,
66, Clarinda 39, 66, Diana 39, 66,
Ellen 39, 66, Henry 39, 66, John 39,
66, Margaret (infant) 39, 66, Mary 39,
66, Nathan 39, 66, Robert 39, 66,
William 39, 66, William Sr 39, 66.

ROGERS - Alfred 68, Alida 68, Minnie

Mae (Wilson) 90, Samuel Emmanuel 68,
Sara 68, Gaston 68, Katherine 68.

ROPER - Abner 69, Darcus 69, Hanna 69,
James 69, Moxais (Muses) (Hamblett) 69,
Rachel Oraton 69, Tans 69, Tillethe 69,
William 69.

ROWE - Elizabeth 42.

RUPP - Clarissa 42.

SCHAFFER - Charles 42.

SCHRENCONGOST - Emma 42, Martin L 42.

SHAFFER - George Paul 40, Paul 40,
Samuel M 40.

SHARP - James Eales 20.

SHEASLEY Clara 42.

SINCLAIR - Annie 70, Emma 70, Eunice
70, Hattey 70, Hector 70, Hugh Crige
21, John 70, Julia 70, Walter Brown 70.

SKAINS - Adam Jr. 70 Adam 708, Charner
70, Francis 70, James 70, Julia 70,
Maria 70, Salina 70, Sarah 70, Thomas
70, Vardell 70, William M 70.

SKIPPER - Mary Cleveland 64.

SMITH - Andrew 71, Andrew Jackson 71,
Aura 71, Carey 71, Charlotte 28, Cheryl
28, Curtis Ross 28, Cynthia 71, David
72, Dicy 71, Douglas MacArthur 72,
Emily 71, George 71, Iris Lorraine
Stewart (Clark) 28, John 71, Johnn 28,
Loran 28, Marvin 28, Mary 71 Maggie 71,
Mike 27, Rebecca 71, Robert 71, Sally
Sizemore 71, Samantha 71, Sara 71, Sara
(Baker) 71, Sarah 71, Sarah Nixon 60,

Thomas 72, Thomas Hamilton 71, Willaim 71.

SNYDER - Alice 41, Annie (Adams) 41, Clara 40, Clara (Sheasley) 41, Clarissa (Rupp) 41, Elizabeth J 41, Elizabeth (Rowe) 41, Emma (Schrencongost) 41, George W 41, Iva (Beck) 40, John Hawke 40, Lucy 41, Mary C 41, Samuel M. 40, Samuel Sylvester 41, Samuel Jr 40, Susan 41, William 41.

STALCUP - Elmer Ellsworth 74, Lottie Leone (Gamble) 74.

STONE - Elizabeth 61.

STOUT - Mary Lovina 23, ? 38.

TECUMSEH 8.

TERRELL - Bearny 75, ? Carter 75, William Mack 75.

TERRY - Nellie 7.

THOMAS - Pauline Michelle Thomas 44, Terrell John 44.

TILLUS - Ella Wilson (Merritt) 90.

TUCKER - Elizabeth (Yahula) 77, George 92, Mary 62, 77, 92, Mary Thomas 77, Thomas 77, 92, Others 77.

TUTEN - Burl R. 77, Cynthia 77, Cynthia Rosela 33, Eliza ? 75, Elizabeth 75, ? 75, Henry 77.

TYRE - Lucinda 29.

WHITE - Joseph White 56, William 56.

WHITMAN - Matilda (Wilson) 90.

WILDER - John Andrew Jackson 76, 78,
Charles 78, Edwin 78, Katie Avera 69,
Linton 78, Mathew 52, Pearl Urshell
(Ash) (Rogers) 8, Samuel 52, William
52, William (II) 76, 89, Willis 50.

WILLIAMS - Nancy 29.

WILSON - Benjamin 90, Beula (Giddeons)
90, Carrie (Langston) 90, Charlie 90,
Ella (Tillus or Merritt) 90, Franklin
90, Gena (Merritt) 90, George 90,
Josephine 90, Louise (Lou) C Gidings
90, Mamie 90, Matilda (Whitman) 90,
Minnie Mae (Rogers) 90, Missouri "Zury"
(Merritt, McCrone) 90, Wynn 90.

WOODRUFF - Amanda 91, Andrew 30,
Benjamin 91, Calvin 30, 91, David 91,
Hiram 30, James 91, John 30, Joshua 91,
Louis 91, Maria 91, Mary 91, Morgan 91,
Vasti 91, William Wirt 30.

WYNN - Garra 39.

X - Jonanen 92.

YAHULA - Charity 24, Elizabeth 77.

ZERRY - Elizabeth 92, Emily 92, John
92, Mary 92, Nancy 92, Nellie 92, Sarah
92, Tom 92, William 92.

INDEX III

RESEARCHERS

Adams, Thomas 35.

Brown, Lori 5, 6, 20-26, 28-32, 35, 53, 70, 75, 90.

Cahaba Tribal Association 7, 24, 37-38, 40, 62, 69, 77, 92.

Carr, Sheila 36-37, 44, 54-55, 67.

Chapman, Betty B (Mrs. Charles) 25.

Daley, Betty 34.

Duffy, Laurie Beth 2-4, 52, 61, 63, 74-75.

Dunn, Kenneth 35.

Eppley, Jeanne L 31, 39, 55, 60, 64-66, 91.

Fulton County Historical Society 20, 22, 56, 58, 76.

Gibson, Nancy 8.

Gilpin, Becky 43.

Jenkins, Lysa 5.

Knighton, Linda 62.

Lemons, Nova A. 23.

Marcinek, Kathy 57.

Mateer, Connie 42.

May, Cathy 8.

Middleton, Cindy 39-40.

Ogle, Sandy 33, 61, 64, 71, 75, 77.

Peace, Lisa M S 28.

Roman, Lew 5-7, 9-19, 22, 26-28, 31-34,
37-38, 42-43, 47-52, 58-59, 64, 66-70,
73, 76-76, 79-88, 90-92.

Sharpe, Nicole 7, 24, 37-38, 40, 62,
69, 77, 92.

Storm, Summer 19.

Talley, Pat 70, 89.

Thomas, G 45.

Wanderling, Candice Louise 62.

Whisler, Frances L 53.

White, Donna 57.

Whitman, Sandra & Patrick C 90.

Wilder, Marian R 8, 17, 20-21, 26, 30,
45, 47, 51-54, 57-59, 63, 65-66, 68-70,
75-76, 78.

Worley, Lisa M 72.

Young, Ellen Erdman 65.